Cooking with Ultrex

By Helen V. Fisher

FISHER
BOOKS™

Publishers: Bill Fisher
                 Helen Fisher
                 Howard Fisher

Editors: Joyce Bush
                 Bill Fisher

Book Production: Deanie Wood
                 Randy Schultz

Drawings: David Fischer
Cover Photos: Mary Ann Krull
                 Balfour Walker Photography

Published by Fisher Books
4239 W. Ina Road, Suite 101
Tucson, Arizona 85741
520/744-6110

Printed in U.S.A.
Printing 10 9 8 7 6 5 4 3 2 1

Originally published as *Cookbook for the 90s*

ISBN 1-55561-163-X

Table of Contents

Acknowledgments

I wish to thank Mable and Gar Hoffman for their generous help with recipe development. Over the past 25 years that I have worked with Mable and Gar, they have been sources of inspiration for me. I feel fortunate to have had their support in the preparation of this book. I also wish to thank Karen Ford Fisher for her help with recipe development and testing. I appreciate the time and effort she dedicated to this project.

Helen Fisher

I'd like to thank my wife, Mary Ann, for putting up with me in the kitchen, and Home Shopping Network, for putting up with me—period.

Art Krull

An Introduction to
Cooking with Ultrex

Everywhere we turn we are being bombarded with new information about health, diet, exercise, foods and nutrition. Health-related newsletters abound, television and radio talk shows encourage us daily to change our ways. A bewildering amount of information is available and it's increasingly difficult to sift through this vast amount of material, picking out what's valid and what's just a fad.

In *Cooking with Ultrex*, I have tried to follow a reasonable course. It's a book that does not go to extremes or make rash promises. It is not a medical book, but a collection of good-tasting recipes and suggestions based upon sound published evidence.

I hope to encourage you to make modest and reasonable changes in food preparation and eating habits that should improve your health. My recipes are low in fat, sugar and sodium, and high in fiber and carbohydrates. I am a firm believer in seasoning with herbs rather than relying on salt. Even though I have used sugar and other sweeteners in recipes, I like the natural flavor to come through without being overpowered by adding too much sweetness.

Food fads come and go very quickly, as do special diets. What we all need to do is examine our own diet and see where we can make lasting changes. Take an honest look at yourself and your eating habits, isn't there room for improvement?

During the last decade, we have become far more aware of the nutritional value of our foods. Historically we cared only for flavor, not really knowing or caring whether we were harming ourselves with overly rich foods. The newer laws requiring labeling of nutritional information give us the facts we previously couldn't get. We can now make a judgment if we want to purchase a particular item based upon its content.

Thanks to breakthroughs made by the medical and nutritional community, we now know fats in our diet greatly affect our health. In no uncertain terms, we are advised to limit our intake of saturated fats and cholesterol. These are mostly found in animal fats like butter or lard which are solid at room temperature. Also to be avoided or limited are egg yolks, whole-milk products with high fat content such as ice cream or cheeses, red meats, and chicken skin. Most vegetable oils are safe to use—the exception being coconut and palm oils. Reducing your intake of saturated fats is a very important dietary change.

Cholesterol has become an everyday topic of conversation. Organ meats, animal fats, egg yolks and some dairy products are all high in cholesterol. We're advised to limit our intake of these foods. It is important to know what your total cholesterol is and adjust your diet to get the number within an acceptable range.

Cooking oils and fats have received a great deal of attention. Seafood and vegetables supply us with the main groups of good unsaturated fats. Whichever oil you choose, use it sparingly. Use additional liquids like broth, wine or juices when braising or stewing dishes. When you use Ultrex nonstick cookware, you need less.

Another term we've learned is omega-3 fatty acid, a substance that appears to help prevent heart disease. Researchers urge us to eat fish at least twice a week.

Studies have been made comparing cuisines of cultures that traditionally use particular oils and fats. For example, the Mediterranean countries have relied upon olive oil and they have less heart disease than Northern Europeans who use large quantities of butter and lard. People who live close to the sea benefit from a diet rich in fish and seafood.

Make an extra effort to enrich your meals with more fruits, cereals, legumes, poultry, vegetables and moderate amounts of nuts. Include fish at least two to three times per week. Limit your intake of lean well-trimmed red meats. You can learn to enjoy lowfat or nonfat milk products.

Food producers are keenly aware of changing appetites and are responding. Great breakthroughs are coming which will aid us in our search for combining "good tasting and good for us." A broad range of foods offering better flavor and fresh appearance are appearing in the refrigerated cases of our markets. Be sure to read the labels for ingredients as well as proper storage and expiration dates. Follow recommended cooking times.

With *Cooking with Ultrex* I hope to convince you—and your tastebuds—that delectable, tasty dishes don't need excessive amounts of fat, sugar and sodium. You can enjoy great flavorful food without guilt. All recipes have the nutritional breakdown to help you get started on a lifetime of delicious and healthy eating.

Helen V. Fisher

Pantry List

Let's make shopping easier for everyone. Here is a list of food items that you should always keep available in the cupboard, refrigerator or freezer. Having the necessary ingredients at hand simplifies trying new recipes.

Bagels, plain
Bran, oat, rice
Canned beans, vegetarian-style
Canned evaporated skimmed milk
Canola oil
Cheeses, lowfat, part skim milk
Chicken breasts, skinless
Chicken broth, lowfat, low-sodium
Chinese five spice
Club soda
Couscous
Crispbreads
Dried beans, black, navy, pinto, lentils
Dried fruits
Dry buttermilk
English muffins, regular or oat
Fish: cod, crab, halibut, herring, orange
    roughy, salmon, scallops, snapper, sole
Fresh fruits in season
Fruit juices: apple, orange, pineapple,
    tomato, etc
Grains: barley oats, couscous, millet,
    oats, rice, whole wheat, quinoa
Herbs
Lowfat mayonnaise
Nonfat cottage cheese
Nonfat dry milk powder

Nonfat milk
Nonfat plain or fruit yogurt
Olive oil
Pasta, no-egg
Peanut butter
Popcorn
Puffed corn, rice, wheat cakes
Rabbit
Rice bran
Rice: brown, white, wild
Salsas
Shellfish: clams, crab, mussels, oysters,
    scallops
Soft diet margarine (with water listed as
    1st ingredient)
Soy sauce, low-sodium
Spices: basil, capers, celery seed,
    cilantro, cinnamon, cloves, curry,
    ginger, lemon pepper, marjoram,
    mustard, nutmeg, paprika
Tortillas, lard-free
Tuna, water-packed
Turkey breasts, skinless
Vegetable cooking spray
Vegetables of all types
Vinegars: apple cider, balsamic, fruit,
    herb, rice, wine

Documentation

Nutrient analysis was calculated using *The Food Processor II Nutrition & Diet Analysis System* software program, version 3.0, copyright 1988, 1990, by ESHA Research. It has a data base of 2400 foods and 30 nutrients and uses USDA and other scientific sources as the data source. Analysis does not include optional ingredients. Only the first choice ingredient is calculated. The higher number is used for the range in servings.

Abbreviations

Because words such as carbohydrates are too long to fit across the bottom of the recipe in chart form, we have abbreviated as follows:

Cal = Calories
Prot = Protein
Carb = Carbohydrates
Fib = Fiber
Tot. Fat = Total Fat
Sat. Fat = Saturated Fat
Chol = Cholesterol

Sample Menus

Breakfast

Pineapple juice
Lowfat cottage cheese
Fresh peaches
Blackberries
Orange-Pecan Muffins
Beverage

Fresh melon slices
Strawberries
Nonfat strawberry yogurt
Date-Pistachio Bread
Beverage

Cranberry juice
Raisin-Oat Bran Pancakes
Canadian bacon
Syrup
Beverage

Lunch

Home-Style Vegetable Soup
Crispbread
Winter Salad
Marmalade Dressing
Beverage

Beef and Bean Burgers
Lettuce
Tomatoes
Whole-wheat buns
Orange wedges
Beverage

Favorite Turkey Chili
Lettuce
Cucumber slices
Toasted English muffin
Mixed fruit cup
Beverage

Dinner

Orange Roughy
Twice-Baked Potatoes
Beets with Raisins
Mixed green salad
House Salad Dressing
Blackberry-Lemon Bars
Beverage

Rosemary-Orange Chicken
Old-Fashioned Potato Salad
Corn on the cob
French bread
Angel food cake
Fresh fruit
Beverage

Stuffed Pork Tenderloin
Brussels Sprouts
Steamed carrots
Mixed green salad
Favorite French Dressing
Baked Apple Delight
Beverage

Appetizers

An appetizer is meant to stimulate your appetite. It can be either a food or drink served before the meal. Allow extra time to enjoy this pleasant way of introducing the meal to come.

Serve the appetizer in a room other than the dining room to set it apart from the dinner. During warm weather appetizers can be served on a porch or patio. This is a relaxed way to introduce guests to one another. Winter's chill causes you to think of a warm, friendly place indoors to begin your entertaining. Consider the living room or den, which is especially nice if it has a fireplace. If your guests enjoy helping, you can begin in the kitchen and invite their participation in preparing or serving. Be guided by the type of guests as well as the occasion.

Fresh vegetables are always appreciated by health-conscious guests. Cut them in attractive shapes and present them with Crab Spread. I like to accompany them with Mediterrean Toast.

Offer a choice of items that will complement the meal. Don't expect a single appetizer will please everyone. If possible, find out some of your guests' favorite foods beforehand and let that be your guide.

Follow a theme and you'll be surprised how easily it works. As a prelude to a Mexican Fiesta, begin with Jícama Canadian Bacon Spread or Avocado Cream and toasted flour-tortilla wedges.

Always present your appetizers in an attractive way. This need not be fancy, but it should be inviting.

Avocado Cream

Capers and pistachios add a surprising flavor to this delicate avocado spread.

1/2 medium avocado, peeled
1/2 cup nonfat cream cheese
1 teaspoon lemon zest
2 teaspoons lemon juice
2 tablespoons pistachios
2 teaspoons cilantro (Chinese parsley)
2 teaspoons capers

Mash avocado and cream cheese together until blended; stir in remaining ingredients. Serve on toasted pita bread or bagels. Makes 1 cup.

Each tablespoon contains:	Cal	Prot	Carb	Fib	Tot. Fat	Sat. Fat	Chol	Sodium
	18	1g	1g	1g	1g	0	0	3mg

Jícama Canadian Bacon Spread

For that final touch at serving time, sprinkle top of spread with finely chopped green onion.

4 oz. Canadian bacon
1 tablespoon white wine vinegar
1 teaspoon chicken bouillon granules
3 (4- to 5-inch) lengths trimmed green onions
(include both green and white portions)
1 cup nonfat or lowfat cottage cheese
1/4 teaspoon celery seed
1/8 teaspoon pepper
4 to 5 oz. jícama, peeled and coarsely chopped

Bake Canadian bacon covered in 350F (175C) oven about 30 minutes. Cool; chop and set aside. In a small custard or measuring cup combine vinegar and chicken granules. Stir until granules are almost dissolved; set aside. In a blender or food processor fitted with a metal blade, combine onion, cottage cheese, celery seed, pepper and vinegar-bouillon mixture. Purée until smooth. Pour purée into 1-quart bowl; stir in bacon and jícama. Cover and refrigerate until serving time. Serve with crackers or party rye bread. Makes about 2 cups.

Each tablespoon contains:	Cal	Prot	Carb	Fib	Tot. Fat	Sat. Fat	Chol	Sodium
	12	2g	1g	0	0	0	2mg	117m

Crab Spread

Good on vegetables, crackers or toasted bagels

1/4 cup nonfat cream cheese, page 1
2 tablespoons nonfat plain yogurt
2 tablespoons nonfat cottage cheese
2 teaspoons lemon juice
2 tablespoons chopped pimiento
3 tablespoons capers
1 teaspoon horseradish
1 green onion, chopped
3 oz. cooked crab
Dill weed to taste

In a small bowl blend cream cheese with yogurt, cottage cheese and lemon juice. Stir in remaining ingredients. Cover and refrigerate until ready to serve.
Serve with toasted pita wedges or crackers. Makes about 1 cup.

Each tablespoon contains:	Cal	Prot	Carb	Fib	Tot. Fat	Sat. Fat	Chol	Sodium
	9	2g	0	0	0	0	5mg	27mg

Mediterranean Toast

Once you've tasted this, you'll prefer it to buttered toast.

6 French bread slices
1/4 cup olive oil
1/2 teaspoon garlic powder
1 tablespoon chopped fresh parsley
1/2 teaspoon dried-leaf oregano
1 teaspoon toasted sesame seeds
1/4 teaspoon paprika

Place bread slices on baking sheet. Preheat broiler or toaster oven. In a small bowl thoroughly combine remaining ingredients until well blended. Brush each slice of bread with mixture. Place under broiler and brown, turn slices and brush again. Return to broiler. Toast until brown. Serve at once. Makes 6 servings.

Each serving contains:	Cal	Prot	Carb	Fib	Tot. Fat	Sat. Fat	Chol	Sodium
	184	4g	18g	1g	11g	2g	0	204mg

Vegetable Dip

Serve with toasted pita bread wedges.

1/2 cup lowfat cottage cheese
1/2 cup nonfat cream cheese
3 sun-dried tomatoes, chopped
2 tablespoons lemon juice or vinegar
2 green onions, chopped
1/4 cup chopped green chiles
1/2 teaspoon dry mustard
2 teaspoons capers
1 teaspoon caper juice
1/4 cup chopped red bell pepper

In a bowl combine all ingredients. Pour into 2-cup serving container; cover and refrigerate several hours before serving. Makes 1-1/4 cups

Each tablespoon contains:	Cal	Prot	Carb	Fib	Tot. Fat	Sat. Fat	Chol	Sodium
	20	1g	2g	0	1g	0	0	27mg

Tuna Dip

Another good way to use small amounts of leftovers. Enjoy this with crispbread and fresh vegetable sticks.

2 tablespoons water-pack tuna, drained
1/2 cup plain nonfat yogurt
1 teaspoon reduced-calorie mayonnaise
1 green onion, chopped
1/4 teaspoon garlic powder
1/4 teaspoon dill weed
1 teaspoon chopped parsley
2 teaspoons pimiento
2 teaspoons prepared pickle relish

In a small bowl combine tuna, yogurt and mayonnaise, breaking tuna into small pieces. Stir in remaining ingredients. Cover and refrigerate until ready to use. Makes 3/4 cup.

Each tablespoon contains:	Cal	Prot	Carb	Fib	Tot. Fat	Sat. Fat	Chol	Sodium
	14	2g	1g	0	0	0	3mg	32mg

Avocado Shrimp Mousse

Present this in an attractive mold.

2 (1/4-oz.) pkgs. unflavored gelatin
3/4 cup chicken broth
3/4 cup skimmed evaporated milk
3 tablespoons lemon juice
1 tablespoon cider vinegar
1 ripe avocado
2 green onions, chopped
1 tablespoon chopped pimiento
1 (6-oz.) can cocktail shrimp
1/4 teaspoon Tabasco sauce or to taste
Salt and lemon pepper to taste
Tomato Salsa, page 66

In a small saucepan sprinkle gelatin over chicken broth. Heat, stirring until gelatin dissolves. Pour broth, milk, lemon juice and vinegar into a food processor or blender. Peel avocado, remove seed and add to mixture with green onion. Process until smooth. Stir in pimiento, shrimp, Tabasco sauce, salt and lemon pepper to taste. Spray a 3-cup mold with vegetable cooking spray. Pour mixture into mold. Cover and refrigerate until set. Serve with Tomato Salsa. Makes 6 (1-/2 cup) servings.

Each serving contains:	Cal	Prot	Carb	Fib	Tot. Fat	Sat. Fat	Chol	Sodium
	129	12g	7g	4g	6g	1g	50mg	90mg

Mediterranean Vegetable Appetizer

Use sun-dried tomatoes without oil for a low-calorie appetizer

2 tablespoons canola or olive oil
1 onion, chopped
1/2 cup sun-dried tomatoes, cut into thin strips
1 carrot, shredded
1 green or yellow pepper, seeded and finely chopped
1 eggplant, minced, peeled
1 teaspoon salt
1/4 teaspoon pepper
1 teaspoon sugar
1 teaspoon red wine vinegar
2 tablespoons chopped fresh cilantro
    (Chinese parsley)
Pita bread rounds

In an Ultrex 12-inch nonstick fry pan heat oil. Add onions; sauté 2 or 3 minutes. Stir in tomatoes, carrot, green or yellow pepper, eggplant, salt, pepper, sugar and vinegar. Simmer 15 to 20 minutes, stirring occasionally, until vegetables are tender. Stir in cilantro. Cut each pita round into 6 or 8 wedges. Let each person spoon vegetable mixture on pita wedges. Makes about 3 cups

Each tablespoon contains:	<u>Cal</u>	<u>Prot</u>	<u>Carb</u>	<u>Fib</u>	Tot. <u>Fat</u>	Sat. <u>Fat</u>	<u>Chol</u>	<u>Sodium</u>
	9	0	1g	0	1g	0	0	45mg

Broccoli Flowers

Make ahead to serve as "pick-up" food at a buffet or picnic.

1 lb. fresh broccoli
1 (5-oz.) pkg. very thinly sliced cooked chicken
**   (about 20 slices)**
2 tablespoons grated Romano cheese
1 tablespoon reduced-calorie mayonnaise
1 tablespoon plain nonfat yogurt
1/2 teaspoon Dijon-style mustard

Trim broccoli; cut flowers and stems into about 20 (3- to 4-inch long) pieces. Cook in boiling water in an Ultrex 2-quart nonstick saucepan about 5 minutes or until tender; drain. While hot sprinkle with cheese. Spread one side of chicken slices with a combination of mayonnaise, yogurt and mustard. Place one length of cooked broccoli in center of each chicken slice. Roll up like a cornucopia with broccoli flower protruding through the open end. Serve warm or cold. Makes 6 servings.

Each serving contains:	Cal	Prot	Carb	Fib	Tot. Fat	Sat. Fat	Chol	Sodium
	73	8g	5g	2g	3g	1g	14mg	201mg

Fruity Barbecue Turkey Pick-ups

A surprise flavor combination that will result in requests for the recipe.

1/2 cup thick hickory smoke barbecue sauce
1 (8-oz.) can jellied cranberry sauce
1 (8-oz.) can crushed pineapple, drained
1/2 teaspoon grated fresh ginger root
1 teaspoon honey
3 cups cubed, skinned, cooked turkey

In an Ultrex 2-quart nonstick saucepan combine barbecue sauce, cranberry sauce, pineapple, ginger root and honey. Stir over low heat until cranberry sauce dissolves. Add turkey and continue cooking until hot. Have wooden picks handy for serving. Makes about 45 turkey pieces.

Each piece with white meat contains:	Cal	Prot	Carb	Fib	Tot. Fat	Sat. Fat	Chol	Sodium
	28	3g	3g	0	0	0	6mg	30mg

Each piece with dark meat contains:	Cal	Prot	Carb	Fib	Tot. Fat	Sat. Fat	Chol	Sodium
	30	3g	3g	0	1g	0	8mg	32mg

Italian Treasure Meatballs

Let your guests discover what is tucked inside.

1/2 lb. select ground beef
1 green onion, chopped
1/4 cup rice bran
1 egg white
2 teaspoons capers
1/2 teaspoon dried-leaf basil
1/2 teaspoon dried-leaf marjoram
1 tablespoon chopped parsley
1 tablespoon tomato sauce
Salt and pepper to taste
20 pimiento-stuffed olives

Preheat oven to 375F (190C). In an Ultrex small mixing bowl combine beef, green onion, rice bran, egg white, capers, basil, marjoram, parsley and tomato sauce. Thoroughly mix ingredients. Take a scant tablespoon full of meat mixture and pat into a patty; press one olive in center. Pinch meat around olive. Place on ungreased cookie sheet. Repeat with remaining olives. Bake 25 to 30 minutes. Makes 20 meatballs.

Each meatball contains:	Cal	Prot	Carb	Fib	Tot. Fat	Sat. Fat	Chol	Sodium
	40	3g	1g	0	3g	1g	10mg	110mg

Soups

Homemade soup brings back memories of home and tasty, nourishing simple meals. Homemade soup is what I grew up with; it wasn't until I was a teenager that I tasted canned soups. They didn't compare to my mother's soups. For something out of the ordinary, serve Chestnut Soup or Artichoke Chowder.

Cold soups are probably enjoyed most during warm weather. We seem to always be looking for the winning combination of something easy to fix, prepare ahead and be well received by all. These are often referred to as a salad you can spoon.

I like to serve cold soups like Cantaloupe, Iced Parsley or Gazpacho on the patio. To keep it chilled on a warm day, place the serving bowl within a larger bowl filled with ice. Have a tray with garnishes, cups and a ladle for stirring and serving. Let each person garnish his own.

Cream soups can help turn a small portion of leftovers, usually vegetables, into a satisfying dish. Served in a cup for a starter or in a bowl for lunch, soup is always welcome. In some Middle European and Far Eastern countries, soup is served for breakfast, a pleasant and nutritious way to start the day.

Albóndigas, a Mexican soup, is an example of a complete meal in a bowl. If this is new to you, be adventuresome and try it.

Artichoke Chowder

A different combination of subtle flavors.

1 tablespoon olive oil
1/2 cup chopped onions
1 cup sliced mushrooms
1 (8-oz.) can artichokes, chopped, drained
2 cups chicken broth
1/2 cup green peas
4 tablespoons all-purpose flour
2 cups evaporated skimmed milk
Salt and pepper to taste

In an Ultrex 3-quart nonstick saucepan heat oil, sauté onions. Add mushrooms, artichokes and broth. Cook about 5 minutes until tender. Add peas. Blend flour in evaporated milk; add to mixture and cook 5 to 7 minutes until slightly thickened. Season to taste with salt and pepper. Makes 5 (1-cup) servings.

Each serving contains:	Cal	Prot	Carb	Fib	Tot. Fat	Sat. Fat	Chol	Sodium
	186	13g	26g	5g	4g	1g	4mg	162mg

Albóndigas

A traditional Mexican soup made with turkey rather than beef.

1/2 lb. skinless turkey, ground
1/4 onion, chopped
1 egg white
1/4 cup quick-cooking rice
8 cups chicken broth
4 cups water
1/4 cup tomato sauce
2 whole roasted chiles, chopped
1 fresh tomato, chopped
1 carrot, julienned
2 green onions, cut in 2-inch lengths
1/4 teaspoon dried-leaf oregano
1/3 cup frozen corn kernels
2 tablespoons fresh chopped cilantro
  (Chinese parsley)

In a small bowl combine turkey, chopped onion, egg white and rice. Take about 1 tablespoon of mixture and form into 1-inch balls. Set aside. In an Ultrex 5-1/2-quart nonstick Dutch oven combine broth, water, tomato sauce, chilies, tomato, carrot, green onions, oregano and corn. Bring mixture to a boil. Add meatballs, reduce heat and simmer about 30 minutes. Add cilantro and cook 5 minutes more. Serve hot. Makes 10 (1-cup) servings.

	Cal	Prot	Carb	Fib	Tot. Fat	Sat. Fat	Chol	Sodium
Each serving contains:	108	11g	6g	1g	4g	1g	16mg	67mg

Dilled Vegetable Soup

This soup is especially good with warm corn bread or Blue Corn Muffins, page 75.

4 cups vegetable broth
1 teaspoon dill weed
Dash of pepper
1-1/2 cups diced potatoes
1/2 cup diced onion
3 carrots, sliced 1/4-inch thick
2 cups sliced zucchini
2 tomatoes, chopped
Salt to taste

Combine broth, dill weed, pepper, potatoes, onion and carrots in an Ultrex 2-quart nonstick saucepan. Bring mixture to full boil, partially cover, reduce heat and simmer 20 minutes. Add zucchini and tomatoes and cook 10 minutes longer or until all vegetables are tender. Salt to taste. Serve hot. Makes 6 (1-cup) servings.

Each serving contains:	Cal	Prot	Carb	Fib	Tot. Fat	Sat. Fat	Chol	Sodium
	107	3g	22g	4g	2g	0	0	19mg

Home-Style Vegetable Soup

Warm and satisfying, a meal that is ideal for a cold day.

1 tablespoon olive oil
1 onion, chopped
2 celery stalks, chopped
2 carrots, sliced
1 zucchini, sliced
1/2 cup canned garbanzo beans (chick peas)
1 (8-oz.) can tomatoes with juice
2 bay leaves
1/2 teaspoon Italian herbs
2 cups chicken broth
1 cup tomato juice
5 cups water
1 tablespoon fresh chopped parsley
1/2 cup fresh sliced mushrooms
2 cups fresh chopped spinach
1 cup cooked pasta

In an Ultrex 5-1/2-quart nonstick Dutch oven heat oil. Sauté onion, celery and carrots. Add zucchini, garbanzo beans, tomatoes with juice, bay leaves, Italian herbs, broth, tomato juice and water. Bring to a boil, reduce heat and cook over medium heat until vegetable are tender, about 30 minutes. Add parsley, mushrooms, spinach and pasta. Cook another 7 to 10 minutes. Remove and discard bay leaves. Makes 8 (1-cup) servings.

Each serving contains:	<u>Cal</u>	<u>Prot</u>	<u>Carb</u>	<u>Fib</u>	Tot. <u>Fat</u>	Sat. <u>Fat</u>	<u>Chol</u>	<u>Sodium</u>
	100	5g	16g	3g	3g	0	0	184mg

Chestnut Soup

Chestnuts can be purchased fresh, canned or vacuum packed.

2 teaspoons canola oil
1/2 onion, chopped
1 carrot, sliced
1 celery stalk, sliced
4 cups chicken broth
1 teaspoon sugar
1 bay leaf
1/4 teaspoon dried-leaf basil
1/8 teaspoon dried-leaf marjoram
24 (1/2 lb.) chestnuts, shelled, roasted
1/2 cup evaporated skimmed milk
3/4 cup marsala, sherry or chicken broth
Salt and pepper to taste

In an Ultrex 5-1/2-quart nonstick Dutch oven heat oil and sauté onion, carrot and celery. Add broth, sugar, bay leaf, basil, marjoram and chestnuts. Simmer until chestnuts are tender, about 25 minutes. Remove and discard bay leaf. Carefully transfer to a food processor or blender and purée mixture. Return to pot and stir in evaporated milk, bring to a boil; add marsala, sherry or chicken broth. Season to taste with salt and pepper. Serve hot or cold. Makes 6 (1-cup) servings.

Each serving contains:	<u>Cal</u>	<u>Prot</u>	<u>Carb</u>	<u>Fib</u>	Tot. <u>Fat</u>	Sat. <u>Fat</u>	<u>Chol</u>	<u>Sodium</u>
	205	6g	29g	6g	3g	1g	2mg	38mg

Lentil Soup

Extra spice adds zest to this hearty dish.

1 cup dried lentils
1/2 onion, chopped
1/2 teaspoon cardamom
1 carrot, sliced
1 celery stalk, sliced
1/2 teaspoon pepper
1 red bell pepper, sliced
1/2 teaspoon cinnamon
4 cups vegetable broth or water
1 (16-oz.) can tomatoes
1 (10-oz.) pkg. frozen broccoli spears
Salt to taste

Rinse and sort lentils. In an Ultrex 5-1/2-quart nonstick Dutch oven combine lentils, onions, cardamom, carrots, celery, pepper, bell peppers, cinnamon and stock. Bring to a boil. Cover, reduce heat and simmer about 30 minutes or until lentils are done. Add tomatoes and broccoli, cook until tender. Salt to taste. Serve hot. Makes 8 (1-cup) servings.

Each serving contains:	Cal	Prot	Carb	Fib	Tot. Fat	Sat. Fat	Chol	Sodium
	149	10g	27g	6g	2g	0	0	111mg

Moussaka Soup

Rich flavor marks this wholesome soup.

1 small eggplant
4 tablespoons olive oil
8 cups broth or lamb stock
1/2 lb. cooked lamb, cubed
1/4 teaspoon salt
1/2 teaspoon dried-leaf oregano
2 large tomatoes, chopped
1/2 cup frozen peas
Grated Parmesan cheese for garnish

Peel eggplant and cut into 1/2-inch cubes. Heat olive oil in an Ultrex 3-quart nonstick saucepan and brown eggplant. Add broth, lamb, salt and oregano. Bring to a full boil. Reduce heat, cover and simmer 5 minutes or until eggplant is very soft. Add tomatoes and peas and cook 2 minutes longer. Serve hot with garnish of grated Parmesan cheese. Makes 5 (1-cup) servings.

Each serving contains:	Cal	Prot	Carb	Fib	Tot. Fat	Sat. Fat	Chol	Sodium
	295	22g	9g	3g	19g	5g	41mg	166mg

Oriental Vegetable Soup

Chicken and pork make a flavorful combination.

1 tablespoon canola oil
1 tablespoon ginger root
1 chicken thigh, skinned
1/2 lb. cubed, fat-trimmed lean pork tenderloin
6 cups chicken broth or stock
3 green onions, chopped
1 (10-oz.) pkg. frozen leaf spinach, thawed
1 (8-1/2-oz.) can water chestnuts, sliced, drained
1/4 lb. fresh mushrooms, sliced
1/4 lb. fresh or 2 cups canned bean sprouts, rinsed, drained
2 teaspoons low-sodium soy sauce
Salt and pepper to taste

Heat oil and ginger root in an Ultrex 5-1/2-quart nonstick Dutch oven. Add chicken and pork, lightly brown. Add broth and green onions, bring to a full boil. Reduce heat and simmer 20 minutes. Add spinach and simmer 3 minutes. Add water chestnuts and mushrooms. Continue cooking 5 minutes or until mushrooms are tender. Add bean sprouts, cover and cook 2 to 3 minutes. Stir in soy sauce. Season to taste with salt and pepper. Serve at once. Makes 12 (1-cup) servings.

Each serving contains:	Cal	Prot	Carb	Fib	Tot. Fat	Sat. Fat	Chol	Sodium
	122	13g	5g	2g	6g	2g	29mg	102mg

Cream of Mushroom Soup

Combine different types of mushrooms for an interesting appearance.

1 lb. fresh mushrooms
3 tablespoons margarine
4 cups vegetable broth or stock
1/2 teaspoon dried-leaf basil
2 cups evaporated skimmed milk
1/2 cup flour
1/4 cup white wine
Salt and pepper to taste

Rub mushrooms with a damp paper towel. Trim mushrooms, slice or chop them in small pieces. In an Ultrex 3-quart nonstick saucepan melt margarine, add mushrooms. Stirring frequently cook mushrooms until lightly brown. Add vegetable broth and basil. Heat to boiling, simmer gently 30 minutes. Remove pan from heat. Blend evaporated milk and flour together; add to mixture. Return pan to heat; stir and simmer until soup thickens. Add wine. Do not allow soup to boil again. Season to taste with salt and pepper. Serve hot. Makes 6 (1-cup) servings.

Each serving contains:	**Cal**	**Prot**	**Carb**	**Fib**	**Tot. Fat**	**Sat. Fat**	**Chol**	**Sodium**
	215	11g	29g	3g	6g	1g	3mg	172mg

Cantaloupe Cooler

This soup tends to separate, so stir well before serving.

1 medium cantaloupe (2 lb.)
1-1/2 cups orange juice
1/4 teaspoon salt
1/4 teaspoon ground ginger
1 tablespoon lime juice
1 (5-1/3-oz.) can sweetened condensed milk
Fresh mint sprigs for garnish
1 lime, thinly sliced, for garnish

Cut cantaloupe in half. Remove peel and seeds; slice in wedges and chop. Put cantaloupe and remaining ingredients in blender or food processor, purée until smooth. Refrigerate several hours.   Stir before serving. Serve cold with garnish of fresh mint or lime slices. Makes 8 (1/2-cup) servings.

Each serving contains:	Cal	Prot	Carb	Fib	Tot. Fat	Sat. Fat	Chol	Sodium
	122	3g	25g	1g	2g	1g	6mg	101mg

Iced Parsley Soup

Your family or guests will welcome a pretty, cool soup to begin a meal.

3 tablespoons margarine
1 medium onion, peeled and chopped
3 cups chicken broth or stock
1/8 teaspoon ground pepper
1 cup plain nonfat yogurt
1 cup chopped fresh parsley
4 teaspoons toasted slivered almonds for garnish

Heat margarine in an Ultrex 2-quart nonstick saucepan. Sauté onion; add chicken broth and pepper. Heat to simmering, cook 5 minutes. Cool slightly. Pour onion-broth mixture into blender or food processor. Add yogurt and purée. Stir in parsley. Refrigerate several hours. Serve cold. Garnish with almonds. Makes 8 (1/2-cup) servings.

	Cal	Prot	Carb	Fib	Tot. Fat	Sat. Fat	Chol	Sodium
Each serving contains:	76	4g	5g	1g	5g	1g	1mg	78mg

Pumpkin Spice Soup

Prepare this in the morning and enjoy it for lunch or dinner.

1 (16-oz.) can pumpkin
2 (13-oz.) cans evaporated skimmed milk
1 tablespoon molasses
1/2 cup light corn syrup
1/2 teaspoon salt
1/2 teaspoon pumpkin-pie spice
Nutmeg for garnish

Place all ingredients in a 2-1/2- to 3-quart mixer bowl. Beat until well blended. Refrigerate several hours. Stir before serving. Sprinkle with nutmeg for garnish. Makes 8 (3/4-cup) servings.

Each serving contains:	Cal	Prot	Carb	Fib	Tot. Fat	Sat. Fat	Chol	Sodium
	154	7g	32g	1g	0	0	4mg	252mg

Sweet and Spicy Carrot Soup

If you prefer a sweeter taste, add 2 teaspoons sugar before chilling.

1-1/2 cups cold water
1/2 teaspoon salt
1 (16-oz.) pkg. frozen carrots
1-1/2 cups orange juice
1/2 teaspoon nutmeg
1 cup chicken broth
1 orange, thinly sliced for garnish
Mint sprigs for garnish

Combine water, salt and carrots in an Ultrex 3-quart nonstick saucepan; cover and bring to a boil. Reduce heat, simmer carrots 8 to 10 minutes or until carrots are very soft. Remove from heat and let cool. In a blender or food processor purée carrots and cooking liquid. In a large bowl combine puréed carrots with orange juice, nutmeg and broth; mix well. Cover bowl and refrigerate 2 hours or until well chilled. Serve cold with garnish of fresh orange slice and mint sprig. Makes 8 servings.

Each serving contains:	Cal	Prot	Carb	Fib	Tot. Fat	Sat. Fat	Chol	Sodium
	47	2g	10g	2g	0	0	0	167mg

Zucchini Cooler

Here's another way to prepare versatile zucchini.

3 medium zucchini
2 cups beef broth or stock
1/2 teaspoon dill weed
1/8 teaspoon garlic powder
1 cup plain nonfat yogurt
1 cup evaporated skimmed milk
Raw zucchini slices for garnish
Chopped pimiento for garnish
Parsley for garnish
Salt and pepper to taste

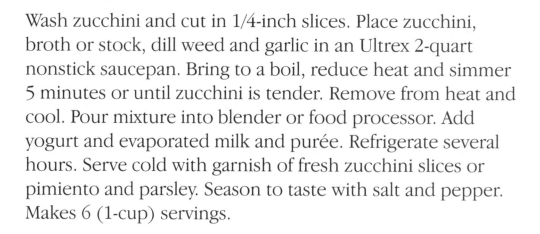

Wash zucchini and cut in 1/4-inch slices. Place zucchini, broth or stock, dill weed and garlic in an Ultrex 2-quart nonstick saucepan. Bring to a boil, reduce heat and simmer 5 minutes or until zucchini is tender. Remove from heat and cool. Pour mixture into blender or food processor. Add yogurt and evaporated milk and purée. Refrigerate several hours. Serve cold with garnish of fresh zucchini slices or pimiento and parsley. Season to taste with salt and pepper. Makes 6 (1-cup) servings.

Each serving contains:	Cal	Prot	Carb	Fib	Tot. Fat	Sat. Fat	Chol	Sodium
	70	7g	10g	1g	0	0	3mg	79mg

Instant Vichyssoise

Cool and creamy, topped with a sprinkle of chives.

2-1/2 cups chicken broth
1 teaspoon instant minced onion
Prepared instant mashed potatoes for 4 servings
1-1/2 cups evaporated skimmed milk
Pepper to taste
Chopped chives for garnish
Fresh parsley for garnish

Combine broth and onion in an Ultrex 2-quart nonstick saucepan and heat to boiling. Remove pan from heat and stir in potatoes. Cover; let stand a few minutes to allow potatoes to absorb liquid. Add evaporated milk and pepper, stir well until smooth and creamy. Cover and refrigerate several hours. Serve cold with garnish of chives or fresh parsley. Makes 8 (1/2-cup) servings.

Each serving contains:	Cal	Prot	Carb	Fib	Tot. Fat	Sat. Fat	Chol	Sodium
	110	6g	13g	0	4g	1g	3mg	238mg

Chilled Avocado with Crab Soup

Transform these few ingredients into a great starter.

2 large ripe avocados
4-1/2 cups chicken broth
1-1/2 cups evaporated skimmed milk
1 tablespoon lemon juice
1 (6-oz.) pkg. frozen crab meat, thawed and drained
Salt and pepper to taste

Peel, remove pits and chop avocados. In a blender combine avocados with broth, evaporated milk and lemon juice; purée. Reserve a few large pieces of crab meat for garnish. Stir remaining crab into puréed avocado mixture. Refrigerate several hours. Season with salt and pepper to taste. Serve cold. Garnish with reserved crab. Makes 6 (1-cup) servings.

Each serving contains:	**Cal**	**Prot**	**Carb**	**Fib**	**Tot.** **Fat**	**Sat.** **Fat**	**Chol**	**Sodium**
	221	16g	17g	10g	11g	2g	28mg	172mg

Salads

Salads play a variety of roles. They can be served as an appetizer, main dish, side dish or a palate cleanser after the entrée. Whichever you choose, be certain to include at least one per day.

Today there is a wonderful selection of greens to choose from. While they have subtle differences in flavor, they have vibrant color differences. For more robust flavor use romaine or chicory (curly endive), which is even stronger—almost pungent. Do not confuse it with Belgian endive, an almost white, small, slender head, which is described as pleasantly bitter. For added interest include contrasting colors like red leaf lettuce or the beautiful radiccio (Italian chicory) whose white veins contrast the deep-red leaves. Generally these eye-catching ingredients are more expensive, but when used sparingly for special occasions you'll find they are worth it.

Three interesting, rather unattractive beige roots are jicama, Jerusalem artichokes (sunchokes) and celery root (celeriac). Peel away the outer inedible coating and discover a white, crunchy, moist interior. Sliced, cubed or grated, they add interest to any salad.

More familiar roots used in cooking stews and soups—turnip, kohlrabi and rutabaga (swede)—are also delicious in salads. Once again, peel before eating. My parents always raised kohlrabi in our garden. When it was young and tender we enjoyed eating it raw.

Edible flowers such as nasturtium, borage, squash blossoms, pansies, rose petals and pot marigold (calendula) can transform your salad into a spectacular dish.

Garnishing is that extra touch that is noticed and welcomed by all, so save your prettiest sprig of fresh herbs for the place of honor.

Barbecue Bean Salad

A wonderful way to use your leftover beans.

1 bunch fresh spinach or salad mixed greens
1 cup Barbecued Beans, page 94
1 zucchini, sliced
1 tomato, chopped
1/4 lb. jícama, cut in sticks
1 tablespoon lemon juice
1 tablespoon chopped parsley

Rinse spinach or salad greens and pat dry. Line salad plates with spinach or mixed greens. Combine beans with zucchini, tomato, jícama and lemon juice. Divide evenly over spinach, sprinkle with parsley. Makes 6 servings.

Each serving contains:	Cal	Prot	Carb	Fib	Tot. Fat	Sat. Fat	Chol	Sodium
	47	2g	10g	2g	0	0	0	35mg

Italian Garbanzo Salad

Prepare this salad any time. I think it's best as a summer lunch.

2 tablespoons canola oil
2 tablespoons sun-dried tomatoes, chopped
1/2 teaspoon dried-leaf oregano
2 tablespoons chopped fresh parsley
2 green onions, chopped
1/2 cup green bell pepper, sliced
1/4 cup lemon juice
1 (15-oz.) can garbanzo beans, rinsed and drained
1-1/2 cups cooked pasta
10 small pimiento-stuffed olives, sliced
1 tomato, chopped

Heat oil in an Ultrex 8-inch nonstick fry pan; sauté sun-dried tomatoes, oregano, parsley, green onions and green pepper slices. Mix in lemon juice, garbanzo beans, pasta and olives. Stir and toss with tomatoes. Serve warm or chilled. Makes 8 (1/2-cup) servings.

Each serving contains:	Cal	Prot	Carb	Fib	Tot. Fat	Sat. Fat	Chol	Sodium
	183	6g	24g	5g	8g	1g	0	123mg

Green Bean-Potato Salad

The Italians inspired my selection of ingredients.

2 cups green beans, cooked
1 cup (1/2 lb.) fresh mushrooms, sliced
2 cups sliced, peeled, cooked potatoes
1/2 cup chopped celery
3 green onions, chopped
1/4 red bell pepper, chopped
1/4 cup raisins
1/4 cup cooked whole-kernel corn
2 tablespoons capers
2 tablespoons pine nuts
1/3 cup Italian Dressing, page 55

In a large salad bowl combine all ingredients. Cover and refrigerate at least 4 hours before serving. Makes 6 (1-cup) servings.

Each serving contains:	Cal	Prot	Carb	Fib	Tot. Fat	Sat. Fat	Chol	Sodium
	130	3g	20g	3g	6g	1g	0	18mg

White Bean Salad

Serve in radiccio leaves, they make attractive cups for the salad.

**1 (16-oz.) can white kidney beans (cannellini),
   or 1 cup cooked small white beans, drained
1 (6-oz.) can water-pack tuna, drained
1 cup sliced green bell pepper
1/2 sweet red onion, chopped
2 celery stalks, sliced
1 large tomato, chopped
1 tablespoon chopped fresh parsley
1/2 cup Italian Dressing, page 55**

Rinse drained beans with water and drain again. In a salad bowl stir all ingredients together. Cover and chill before serving. Makes 8 servings.

Each serving contains:	Cal	Prot	Carb	Fib	Tot. Fat	Sat. Fat	Chol	Sodium
	151	12g	18g	5g	4g	1g	12mg	91mg

Old-Fashioned Potato Salad

Old-fashioned salad made healthier with yogurt.

3 cups cooked new potatoes
2 tablespoons chopped green olives
1/2 cup cooked peas
1/4 teaspoon dried dill weed
1 tablespoon chopped parsley
1/2 teaspoon sugar
1/4 cup chopped green onions
2 tablespoons lemon juice
2 tablespoons reduced-calorie mayonnaise
1/3 cup nonfat plain yogurt
2 tablespoons chopped chives
1/4 cup chopped celery
Salt and pepper to taste
1 sprig fresh dill for garnish

Slice potatoes and place in a large bowl. Add remaining ingredients; toss gently to combine. Garnish with sprig of fresh dill. Serve either warm or cold. Makes 4 servings.

Each serving contains:	Cal	Prot	Carb	Fib	Tot. Fat	Sat. Fat	Chol	Sodium
	148	4g	28g	3g	3g	0	2mg	236mg

Confetti Salad

Our colorful picnic slaw.

> **3 cups shredded red cabbage**
> **1 apple, cored, sliced**
> **1/2 cup dried currants**
> **1/4 cup cooked whole-kernel corn, drained**
> **1/2 cup green grapes**
> **2 celery stalks, sliced**
> **2/3 cup Balsamic Herb Dressing, page 50**

In a salad bowl mix cabbage, apple, currants, corn, grapes and celery. Pour Balsamic Herb Dressing over and toss to coat. Makes 6 servings.

Each serving contains:	Cal	Prot	Carb	Fib	Tot. Fat	Sat. Fat	Chol	Sodium
	199	2g	21g	3g	14g	2g	0	21mg

Couscous Fruit Salad

A nice way to introduce couscous, accented with tropical flavors.

1-1/4 cups pineapple-orange juice
1/4 teaspoon cinnamon
1/4 teaspoon mace
1 cup couscous
1 cup pineapple chunks, drained
1 banana, sliced
2 teaspoons lemon juice
1/2 avocado, chopped
3 tablespoons toasted almonds

Place pineapple-orange juice, cinnamon and mace in an Ultrex 1-quart nonstick saucepan; heat until boiling. Stir in couscous. Cover and remove from heat. Let stand 5 minutes. Spoon in pineapple chunks. Pour mixture into a serving bowl. Top with banana slices. Sprinkle banana slices with lemon juice. Top with avocado and almonds. Makes 6 servings.

	Cal	Prot	Carb	Fib	Tot. Fat	Sat. Fat	Chol	Sodium
Each serving contains:	176	4g	30g	4g	5g	1g	0	5mg

Fennel Spinach Salad

A pleasing combination of fresh greens and dried fruits. Fennel is also called Sweet Anise or Finnocio.

1/3 cup chopped dried white figs
1/3 cup chopped dates
1/2 cup Italian Dressing, page 55
1 bunch fresh spinach
1/4 head red-leaf lettuce
1 fennel (sweet anise) bulb, trimmed and sliced
2 tablespoons pine nuts

Place figs and dates in a small bowl, cover with Italian Dressing. Wash spinach and lettuce, remove stems; pat leaves dry with paper towels. Tear into pieces. Place spinach and fennel slices in a serving bowl. Top with fruits, dressings and pine nuts; toss to combine. Makes 4 servings.

Each serving contains:	Cal	Prot	Carb	Fib	Tot. Fat	Sat. Fat	Chol	Sodium
	320	6g	42g	9g	18g	3g	0	77mg

Greek Salad

The Greeks dip their bread into the dressing rather than buttering it.

3 tomatoes, chopped
2 cucumbers, sliced
1/2 green bell pepper, sliced
1/2 onion, chopped
4 radishes, sliced
1 tablespoon capers
1/2 teaspoon dried-leaf oregano
2 tablespoons wine vinegar
4 tablespoons olive oil
1 oz. feta cheese, crumbled
Lettuce leaves, torn in bite-size pieces
12 black Greek olives

In a large bowl combine all ingredients. Chill and serve with a crusty French bread. Makes 4 servings.

Each serving contains:	Cal	Prot	Carb	Fib	Tot. Fat	Sat. Fat	Chol	Sodium
	205	3g	13g	4g	17g	3g	6mg	210mg

Island Slaw

The addition of fruit is a nice surprise.

3 tablespoons vinegar
3 tablespoons lemon juice
1/2 teaspoon pepper
3 tablespoons sugar
1 teaspoon caraway seeds
1/4 cup dried currants
1/4 cup chopped dates
1 cup sliced celery
4 cups shredded cabbage
1/2 cup crushed pineapple

In a cup combine vinegar, lemon juice, pepper, sugar, caraway seeds, currants and dates. Let stand 15 minutes. In a large bowl combine remaining ingredients and toss with dressing. Serve at once. Makes 6 servings.

Each serving contains:	Cal	Prot	Carb	Fib	Tot. Fat	Sat. Fat	Chol	Sodium
	81	1g	21g	2g	0	0	0	17mg

Mediterranean Salad

A new way to toss a salad and dressing.

1 large tomato, seeded and diced
1 large green pepper, seeded and diced
1 large cucumber, seeded and diced
6 radishes, diced
1 tablespoon chopped Italian parsley
12 small, pitted green olives
2 teaspoons red wine vinegar
1/2 teaspoon black pepper
Bibb lettuce

Combine all vegetables and parsley in bowl. Spray with olive-oil vegetable cooking spray. Mix well. Sprinkle vegetables with vinegar and black pepper. Toss well. Chill about 1 hour. Serve over lettuce leaves. Makes 6 servings.

Each serving contains:	Cal	Prot	Carb	Fib	Tot. Fat	Sat. Fat	Chol	Sodium
	25	1g	4g	1g	1g	0	0	192mg

Sunshine Salad

Carrots and orange add a dash of color and flavor to this eye-appealing salad.

1/4 cup vinegar
1/4 cup canola oil
1/3 cup sugar
1 teaspoon dry mustard
1/2 teaspoon celery seed
1 teaspoon grated onion
1/4 teaspoon salt
4 cups shredded red or green cabbage
1 carrot, shredded
1 medium orange, peeled, cut into small chunks

In an Ultrex 1-quart nonstick saucepan combine vinegar, oil, sugar, dry mustard, celery seed, onion and salt. Stir over medium heat until sugar dissolves. Cool to room temperature. Combine cabbage, carrot and orange in large bowl. Pour dressing over; toss to coat. Makes 6 to 7 servings.

Each serving contains:	<u>Cal</u>	<u>Prot</u>	<u>Carb</u>	<u>Fib</u>	Tot. <u>Fat</u>	Sat. <u>Fat</u>	<u>Chol</u>	<u>Sodium</u>
	129	1g	15g	2g	8g	0	0	87mg

Three-Pepper Salad

Brighten your meal with this great salad.

1/2 cup House Salad Dressing, page 54
1 cup fresh lima beans, cooked
1 red bell pepper, julienned
1 yellow or orange bell pepper, julienned
1 green bell pepper, julienned
2 green onions, chopped
1 cup mushrooms, sliced
1 tablespoon chopped fresh basil or 1 teaspoon
 dried-leaf basil
Spinach or Romaine lettuce leaves
1 tablespoon toasted pumpkin seeds

Pour House Salad Dressing over lima beans and marinate at least 1 hour. Add remaining ingredients, except spinach leaves and pumpkin seeds, tossing to combine. Line salad bowl with spinach or Romaine lettuce leaves. Place salad on top of leaves. Sprinkle with pumpkin seeds. Makes 4 to 6 servings.

Each serving contains:	Cal	Prot	Carb	Fib	Tot. Fat	Sat. Fat	Chol	Sodium
	135	3g	12g	4g	9g	1g	0	21mg

Zucchini Salad

Cucumber can be substituted if zucchini is not available.

1 zucchini, thinly sliced
1 red onion, thinly sliced
2 tomatoes, thinly sliced
3 tablespoons olive oil
1 tablespoon wine vinegar or apple cider
2 tablespoons lemon juice
1/4 teaspoon garlic powder
1/4 teaspoon dill weed
1 tablespoon chopped fresh basil or 1 teaspoon
   dried-leaf basil
1 tablespoon roasted, unsalted sunflower seeds

In a salad bowl alternate slices of zucchini, red onion and tomatoes. In a cup blend oil, wine vinegar or apple cider, lemon juice, garlic powder, dill weed and basil. Pour over zucchini mixture and sprinkle with sunflower seeds. Cover and chill before serving. Makes 4 to 6 servings.

Each serving contains:	**Cal**	**Prot**	**Carb**	**Fib**	**Tot. Fat**	**Sat. Fat**	**Chol**	**Sodium**
	90	1g	5g	1g	8g	1g	0	5mg

Summer Fruit Salad

A cool satisfying lunch or a special breakfast treat.

1 cantaloupe
1 cup reduced-fat ricotta cheese
1/4 cup orange juice
1 banana, sliced
2 kiwis, sliced, peeled
16 strawberries, halved
Honey Dressing, page 52, or Marmalade Dressing, page 53

Peel melon and cut into slices. Divide them equally on 4 plates. In a small bowl stir cheese and orange juice together. Fold in banana slices. Mound cheese mixture on top of melon slices. Arrange kiwi slices attractively. Garnish with strawberries. Top with Honey or Marmalade Dressing. Makes 4 servings.

Each serving without dressing contains:	**Cal**	**Prot**	**Carb**	**Fib**	**Tot. Fat**	**Sat. Fat**	**Chol**	**Sodium**
	211	9g	34g	5g	6g	3g	19mg	92mg

Winter Salad

Grapefruit and apples make a splendid team.

Lettuce or spinach leaves
1 grapefruit, peeled, cut in segments
1 apple, cut in eighths
1/2 cup Marmalade Dressing, page 53
1/2 cup green grapes
2 tablespoons pomegranate seeds or raspberries

Arrange lettuce or spinach leaves on four salad plates. Top with alternating grapefruit segments and apple slices. Drizzle 2 tablespoons Marmalade Dressing over each salad. Top with green grapes and pomegranate seeds or raspberries. Makes 4 servings.

Each serving with dressing contains:	<u>Cal</u>	<u>Prot</u>	<u>Carb</u>	<u>Fib</u>	Tot. <u>Fat</u>	Sat. <u>Fat</u>	<u>Chol</u>	<u>Sodium</u>
	156	2g	40g	2g	0	0	0	21mg

Chicken Salad

A cool, light main-dish salad. Serve with Mediterranean Toast, page 4, and a cold drink.

1 cup cubed, skinned, cooked chicken
1 apple, sliced
1 cucumber, sliced, peeled
1/2 cantaloupe, cubed, peeled
1/2 cup blueberries
1/2 cup green seedless grapes
1/4 head lettuce, torn in bite-size pieces
1/3 cup House Salad Dressing, page 54

Chill all ingredients. Combine all salad ingredients in a large bowl. Toss with dressing. Spoon onto serving plates. Makes 4 servings.

Each serving with white meat contains:	<u>Cal</u>	<u>Prot</u>	<u>Carb</u>	<u>Fib</u>	Tot. <u>Fat</u>	Sat. <u>Fat</u>	<u>Chol</u>	<u>Sodium</u>
	207	10g	21g	3g	10g	1g	22mg	44mg

Each serving with dark meat contains:	<u>Cal</u>	<u>Prot</u>	<u>Carb</u>	<u>Fib</u>	Tot. <u>Fat</u>	Sat. <u>Fat</u>	<u>Chol</u>	<u>Sodium</u>
	219	9g	21g	3g	12g	1g	25mg	47mg

Shrimp & Scallop Salad

If cantaloupe is not available, substitute papaya or mango slices.

Lettuce or spinach leaves
1 cantaloupe, peeled, sliced
1/2 cup cooked shrimp
1/2 cup cooked scallops
2 celery stalks, sliced
1 green onion, finely chopped
1 cucumber, sliced
12 cherry tomatoes
2 limes or lemons

Line 4 plates with lettuce or spinach leaves. Place 1/4 of cantaloupe slices on each plate. Add a mound of shrimp and scallops, top with celery and green onion. Place cucumbers and cherry tomatoes on the side. Cut limes or lemons into wedges; place on plates. Let each person squeeze wedges over salad as they desire. Makes 4 servings.

Each serving contains:	Cal	Prot	Carb	Fib	Tot. Fat	Sat. Fat	Chol	Sodium
	115	9g	19g	4g	1g	0	34mg	94mg

Turkey Melba Salad

Fresh berries make a pretty as well as tasty addition.

1 bunch spinach
1 celery stalk, sliced
1 cup cubed, skinned, cooked turkey
2 fresh peaches, peeled, sliced
1 cup fresh raspberries or strawberries
2 tablespoons toasted pecans
Honey Dressing, page 52,
   or House Salad Dressing, page 54

Thoroughly rinse spinach. Pat dry and tear into bite-size pieces. In a salad bowl combine spinach, celery, turkey, peaches, raspberries or strawberries and pecans. Toss together gently with Honey or House Salad Dressing.

Or line 6 salad plates with spinach; arrange celery, turkey and peaches on top. Scatter with raspberries or strawberries and top with Honey or House Salad Dressing. Sprinkle with pecans. Makes 6 servings.

Each serving with white meat contains:	**Cal**	**Prot**	**Carb**	**Fib**	**Tot. Fat**	**Sat. Fat**	**Chol**	**Sodium**
	81	8g	7g	3g	3g	0	16mg	35mg

Each serving with dark meat contains:	**Cal**	**Prot**	**Carb**	**Fib**	**Tot. Fat**	**Sat. Fat**	**Chol**	**Sodium**
	88	8g	7g	3g	4g	1g	20mg	39mg

Dressings, Relishes & Sauces

Even though a salad or entrée is complete in itself, often the addition of a complementary dressing, relish or sauce adds that special taste which makes it memorable.

I choose a light-flavored oil for most cooking, but will use a more robust olive oil where I feel it enhances the flavor of the dish or dressing. Walnut and avocado oils make wonderful salad dressings.

Enhance a simple vinaigrette by making your own flavored vinegars. This requires some forethought because the best results come after allowing flavors to blend at least three weeks. Experiment with both herb and fruit combinations. A few minutes' preparation can result in giving your dressing that personal touch.

The *Chipotle* chile may be new to you. This brown, plump chile has a distinctive smoky flavor. Canned chipotle chilies are found in the specialty or Mexican food section of your market. Fresh or dried varieties can be purchased in produce markets featuring Hispanic ingredients.

When introducing spicy salsas, serve small portions, for the combinations can surprise the palate. Flavorful salsas or relishes can accent your broiled chicken, fish or meat entrée. Served as a side dish, they brighten any meal, and at our house we enjoy them with sandwiches.

I also offer my own easy uncooked Pineapple Salsa that can be made with other fruits such as papaya, peach, apricot or pear.

The addition of a relish like Taste-of-the-Tropics or Plum Rhubarb Chutney is a delightful way to add more interest to the meal, as well as a bit more fiber.

Balsamic Herb Dressing

Balsamic vinegar gives this simple dressing that special flavor.

3 tablespoons Balsamic vinegar
2 tablespoons lemon juice
6 tablespoons olive oil
3 garlic cloves, crushed
1/2 teaspoon dry mustard
1/2 teaspoon dried-leaf basil
1/2 teaspoon dried-leaf oregano
1/2 teaspoon paprika

Combine all ingredients in a jar with a tight-fitting lid. Or blend ingredients in a food processor or blender. Store in a covered container. Always shake salad dressing vigorously before using. Makes about 2/3 cup.

Each tablespoon contains:	Cal	Prot	Carb	Fib	Tot. Fat	Sat. Fat	Chol	Sodium
	68	0	1g	0	7g	1g	0	0

Favorite French Dressing

This was chosen as the favorite dressing for mixed green salads.

1/2 cup canola oil
1/4 cup vinegar
2 tablespoons grated onion
2 tablespoons sugar
1/3 cup catsup
1 teaspoon paprika
1 teaspoon pepper
1 tablespoon lemon juice
1/2 teaspoon prepared Dijon-style mustard
2 garlic cloves

Place all ingredients in blender and mix well. Pour into container and cover. Chill before using. Shake vigorously before pouring on salad greens. Makes about 1-1/4 cups.

Each tablespoon contains:	Cal	Prot	Carb	Fib	Tot. Fat	Sat. Fat	Chol	Sodium
	74	0	4g	0	7g	0	0	62mg

Honey Dressing

That extra touch of sweetness for any fruit plate.

1/2 cup honey
1/2 cup lemon juice
3 tablespoons canola oil
Curry powder to taste
Poppy seeds to taste

Combine honey, lemon juice and oil. Add curry powder and poppy seeds to taste. Stir before using. Makes about 1 cup.

Each tablespoon contains:	**Cal**	**Prot**	**Carb**	**Fib**	**Tot. Fat**	**Sat. Fat**	**Chol**	**Sodium**
	57	0	9g	0	3g	0	0	1mg

Marmalade Dressing

Fruit salads or green salads taste better when topped with this tangy dressing.

1/2 cup plain nonfat yogurt
2 tablespoons honey
1/4 teaspoon dry mustard
1/2 cup orange, grapefruit or lime marmalade

In a cup stir all ingredients together until thoroughly combined. Cover and refrigerate until ready to use. Stir before using. Makes about 3/4 cups.

Each tablespoon contains:	Cal	Prot	Carb	Fib	Tot. Fat	Sat. Fat	Chol	Sodium
	51	1g	13g	0	0	0	0	10mg

House Salad Dressing

Make a double recipe and use half as a marinade for cooked vegetables.

1/3 cup canola oil
1/4 cup cider vinegar
1 teaspoon sugar
1 teaspoon dry mustard
1/2 teaspoon paprika
1/2 teaspoon Worcestershire sauce
1 garlic clove, chopped

Combine all ingredients. Let stand at room temperature at least 2 hours. Stir vigorously before using. Makes about 2/3 cup.

Each tablespoon contains:	Cal	Prot	Carb	Fib	Tot. Fat	Sat. Fat	Chol	Sodium
	63	0	1g	0	7g	0	0	11mg

Italian Dressing

Vary the spices to suit your own taste.

1/2 cup olive oil
2 tablespoons cider vinegar
2 tablespoons lemon juice
1 garlic clove
1 green onion, chopped
1/2 teaspoon dried-leaf oregano
1/2 teaspoon dry mustard
2 tablespoons tomato juice

Combine all ingredients in a jar or container with a tight-fitting lid. Shake and let stand an hour before using. Shake vigorously before using. Makes about 1 cup.

Each tablespoon contains:	Cal	Prot	Carb	Fib	Tot. Fat	Sat. Fat	Chol	Sodium
	61	0	0	0	7g	1g	0	7mg

Cucumber-Yogurt Dressing

Make this early in the day and let the flavor develop.

1 cucumber, shredded, peeled, seeded
1/2 cup nonfat plain yogurt
2 tablespoons pine nuts
2 tablespoons capers
1 tablespoon lemon juice
1/2 teaspoon garlic powder
1 tablespoon chopped parsley
Salt and pepper to taste

In a small bowl combine shredded cucumber with remaining ingredients. Cover and chill before serving. Makes about 1-1/4 cups.

Each tablespoon contains:	Cal	Prot	Carb	Fib	Tot. Fat	Sat. Fat	Chol	Sodium
	13	1g	1g	0	1g	0	0	5mg

Green-Chile Mayonnaise

Use as a topping on fish or chicken or as a sandwich spread.

1/2 cup reduced-calorie mayonnaise
2 green onions, chopped
3 whole green chiles, seeded
1/4 teaspoon dried-leaf oregano
1 teaspoon lemon juice

Combine all ingredients in a food processor or blender. Process until thoroughly blended. Refrigerate in a container with a tight-fitting lid. Makes about 1 cup.

Each tablespoon contains:	Cal	Prot	Carb	Fib	Tot. Fat	Sat. Fat	Chol	Sodium
	21	0	2g	0	1g	0	2mg	38mg

Thousand Island Dressing

Reduced-fat dressing to use with mixed greens or seafood salad.

1/3 cup reduced-calorie mayonnaise
1/3 cup nonfat plain yogurt
3 tablespoons chile sauce or catsup
1 tablespoon minced green pepper
1 teaspoon minced chives
1 teaspoon minced pimiento
2 tablespoons sweet-pickle relish
1/4 teaspoon salt
Pepper to taste

In a small bowl combine mayonnaise, yogurt and chile sauce or catsup. Stir in remaining ingredients. Refrigerate in a container with a tight-fitting lid. Makes about 1 cup.

Each tablespoon contains:	Cal	Prot	Carb	Fib	Tot. Fat	Sat. Fat	Chol	Sodium
	20	0	3g	0	1g	0	1mg	118mg

Tomato-Yogurt Sauce

Drained canned tomatoes can be substituted for fresh.

2 large tomatoes, chopped, seeded, peeled
3 tablespoons chopped parsley
1/2 teaspoon Worcestershire sauce
1/2 teaspoon low-sodium soy sauce
1/2 cup nonfat plain yogurt
1 green onion, chopped

In a small bowl combine all ingredients. Cover and refrigerate at least 1 hour for flavors to blend. Makes about 1 cup.

Each tablespoon contains:	Cal	Prot	Carb	Fib	Tot. Fat	Sat. Fat	Chol	Sodium
	8	1g	1g	0	0	0	0	25mg

Taste-of-the-Tropics Relish

Especially good with grilled chicken or Barbecued Turkey Burgers, page 187.

1 fresh papaya, diced and peeled
1 (8-oz.) can crushed unsweetened pineapple
1 teaspoon grated orange peel
1/4 teaspoon grated fresh ginger root
1 jalapeño pepper, seeded and finely chopped
2 tablespoons minced green onions

In a small bowl combine papaya, pineapple with juice, orange peel, ginger, jalapeño pepper and green onions. Refrigerate in a container with a tight-fitting lid. Makes about 2 cups.

Each tablespoon contains:	Cal	Prot	Carb	Fib	Tot. Fat	Sat. Fat	Chol	Sodium
	8	0	2g	0	0	0	0	4mg

Cran-Apple Sauce

Equally good served as a dessert or as a side dish with poultry or pork.

1 cup fresh cranberries
6 large apples, peeled, cored, and coarsely
  chopped
1/2 cup sugar
1/3 cup apple juice
1/4 teaspoon ground mace
1/8 teaspoon ground coriander

Combine ingredients in an Ultrex 3-quart nonstick saucepan. Bring to a boil. Cover and simmer 5 to 10 minutes or until apples are tender. Finely chop in food processor. Cover and refrigerate until cool. Makes about 4 cups.

Each tablespoon contains:	Cal	Prot	Carb	Fib	Tot. Fat	Sat. Fat	Chol	Sodium
	14	0	4g	0	0	0	0	0

Sweet & Sour Sauce

Find out how easy it is to make your own sauce.

1 (8-oz.) can pineapple chunks
3/4 cup reserved pineapple juice
1 tablespoon low-sodium soy sauce
1 tablespoon brown sugar
1 tablespoon cider vinegar
2 tablespoons catsup
1 tablespoon cornstarch
1/2 green bell pepper, cut in 1-inch pieces
1 (4-oz.) jar maraschino cherries, drained

Drain juice from pineapple and set pineapple aside. If necessary add water to make 3/4 cup juice. In an Ultrex 1-quart nonstick saucepan combine juice, soy sauce, brown sugar, vinegar, catsup and cornstarch. Cook, stirring constantly until thickened. Add green pepper, reserved pineapple and cherries. Cook until heated. Serve at once. Makes about 2 cups.

Each tablespoon contains:	Cal	Prot	Carb	Fib	Tot. Fat	Sat. Fat	Chol	Sodium
	11	0	3g	0	0	0	0	44mg

Corn-Tomato Sauce

Orange juice adds extra flavor to tomatoes.

4 cups chopped tomatoes
1 onion, chopped
1 green bell pepper, chopped
1 red bell pepper, chopped
1 chile pepper, chopped
1 tablespoon sugar
1/2 teaspoon salt
1/4 teaspoon ginger
1/4 teaspoon nutmeg
1-1/4 cups orange juice
1 (17-oz.) can whole-kernel corn, drained

In an Ultrex 3-quart nonstick saucepan combine all ingredients except corn. Cook over medium heat about 30 minutes. Stir occasionally. Add corn and cook 5 minutes. Makes about 6 cups.

Each tablespoon contains:	**Cal**	**Prot**	**Carb**	**Fib**	**Tot. Fat**	**Sat. Fat**	**Chol**	**Sodium**
	90	0	2g	0	0	0	0	24mg

Pear & Watermelon Preserve Relish

Accent broiled fish with this tangy mixture.

3 firm, near-ripe pears, chopped, cored, peeled
1 (10-oz.) jar watermelon preserves, chopped
1 apple, chopped, cored, peeled
1/2 onion, chopped
2 tablespoons chopped crystallized ginger
3 tablespoons lemon juice
2 tablespoons raisins
3 tablespoons wine vinegar

In an Ultrex 3-quart nonstick saucepan combine all ingredients. Cover and cook over medium heat about 15 minutes or until pears and apples are tender. Remove from heat. Serve warm or chilled. Makes about 3 cups.

Each tablespoon contains:	Cal	Prot	Carb	Fib	Tot. Fat	Sat. Fat	Chol	Sodium
	27	0	7g	0	0	0	0	1mg

Pineapple Salsa

Be daring and substitute papaya, mango, apricot or cantaloupe for the pineapple.

1 roasted whole chile, chopped, seeded, peeled
2 green onions, chopped
2 tablespoons chopped fresh cilantro
   (Chinese parsley)
1 tablespoon chopped fresh parsley
1 cup fresh or 1 (8-oz.) can pineapple chunks,
   drained

In a small bowl combine all ingredients. Cover and refrigerate at least 20 minutes before serving. Serve as a topping on broiled fish or chicken or as a relish. Makes about 1-1/2 cups.

				Tot.	Sat.		
Each tablespoon contains: <u>**Cal**</u>	<u>**Prot**</u>	<u>**Carb**</u>	<u>**Fib**</u>	<u>**Fat**</u>	<u>**Fat**</u>	<u>**Chol**</u>	<u>**Sodium**</u>
7	0	2g	0	0	0	0	0

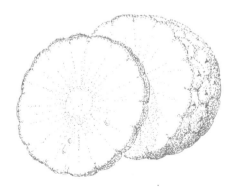

Tomato Salsa

Serve as a dip or topping on Avocado Shrimp Mousse, page 7. Great with any Mexican dish.

1 (8-oz.) can tomato sauce
1/4 cup chopped onion
2/3 cup chopped green chiles
1/4 to 1/2 teaspoon chili powder
2 tomatoes, chopped
1 tablespoon chopped cilantro (Chinese parsley)

Combine all ingredients in a small container. Cover and refrigerate. Let flavor develop 2 to 3 hours before using. Makes about 2 cups.

Each tablespoon contains:	Cal	Prot	Carb	Fib	Tot. Fat	Sat. Fat	Chol	Sodium
	6	0	1g	0	0	0	0	44mg

Tomato Marmalade

Tastier than any you could purchase. Use to top any broiled meat or for a sandwich spread.

4 cups peeled tomatoes
4 cups sugar
1/2 teaspoon salt
1/4 cup vinegar
1 small lemon, thinly sliced
1/2 teaspoon ground cinnamon
1/2 teaspoon ground cloves
1/2 teaspoon red (cayenne) pepper

Combine all ingredients in an Ultrex 5-1/2-quart nonstick saucepan or dutch oven. Let stand 20 minutes. Cook over medium heat, stirring occasionally to prevent sticking. Bring to a boil. Cook about 20 minutes. Pour into hot, sterilized jars and seal at once, or let cool and refrigerate. This can be refrigerated for weeks. Makes 4 to 5 (8-oz.) jars.

Each tablespoon contains:	Cal	Prot	Carb	Fib	Tot. Fat	Sat. Fat	Chol	Sodium
	82	0	21g	0	0	0	0	29mg

Plum Rhubarb Chutney

Add interest and flavor to grilled meats or fish.

1 lb. rhubarb, cut in 1-inch pieces
1 lb. plums, pitted
1 onion, chopped
1/2 cup pitted chopped dates
1 cup vinegar
1-1/2 cups sugar
1 teaspoon ground ginger
1 teaspoon ground allspice

Combine all ingredients in an Ultrex 5-1/2-quart nonstick saucepan or dutch oven. Cook over low heat until mixture becomes jam-like in texture. Cool and spoon into jars. Refrigerate in containers with tight-fitting lids. This keeps under refrigeration for months. Makes about 6 cups.

Each tablespoon contains:	Cal	Prot	Carb	Fib	Tot. Fat	Sat. Fat	Chol	Sodium
	19	0	5g	0	0	0	0	0

Breads

Called the *Staff of Life,* bread is what we all include in our diet each day. For many of us the day begins with juice and toast or muffins. It is difficult to think of not enjoying these regularly. You'll find whole grains can be incorporated in many recipes, whether in loaves, rolls, pancakes or muffins.

Quick breads and muffins are gaining in popularity because they are easy to prepare and take little time to bake. Hot muffins can be baking while you prepare the rest of dinner. The little extra effort is always appreciated.

With so many in the work force, many of us no longer have the time required to make yeast breads. But when you have a little extra time, try one of my yeast breads. With a little practice and patience, you'll gain confidence to experiment and personalize the recipes. Simply add your favorite herbs and enjoy.

Pancakes make a wonderful light supper, as well as special breakfast or brunch fare. They are delightfully tender when made with yogurt or cottage cheese. Flavor and interest can be increased by adding your favorite chopped nuts or dried fruit. My Walnut Sweet Potato Pancakes are an example. Try topping them with fresh fruit and powdered sugar or with fruit syrups.

If you enjoy wholesome multi-grain breads but are not inclined to make your own, be selective when shopping. Read the ingredient lists, avoiding products that include whole eggs or undesirable fat. More and more "good-fat" breads are appearing in response to customers' wants and needs.

Buttermilk-Pistachio Pancakes

Tender pancakes with delicious little green nuggets.

1 cup all-purpose flour
2 tablespoons brown sugar
1 tablespoon baking powder
1/2 tablespoon baking soda
1 cup lowfat buttermilk
1 teaspoon vanilla extract
2 tablespoons canola oil
2 egg whites, beaten
3 tablespoons chopped pistachios

Preheat griddle or electric fry pan. Stir together flour, brown sugar, baking powder and baking soda in an Ultrex medium mixing bowl. Beat in buttermilk, vanilla extract, oil and egg whites. Add chopped pistachios. Lightly spray griddle with vegetable cooking spray. Pour 1/4 cup batter for each pancake. Cook 2 to 3 minutes until bubbles appear and surface looks dry. Turn; cook 2 to 3 minutes until browned. Makes 12 (3-inch) pancakes.

Each pancake contains:	Cal	Prot	Carb	Fib	Tot. Fat	Sat. Fat	Chol	Sodium
	86	3g	11g	0	4g	0	1mg	216mg

Raisin-Oat Bran Pancakes

Start the day with these raisin treats.

1 cup all-purpose flour
1/2 cup oat bran
1 tablespoon sugar
1 teaspoon baking soda
2 teaspoons baking powder
1/2 teaspoon cinnamon
1/2 cup egg substitute or 4 egg whites, beaten
1-1/2 cups lowfat buttermilk
2 tablespoons canola oil
1/2 teaspoon vanilla extract
1/4 cup raisins

Spray a non-stick griddle with vegetable cooking spray. Preheat griddle. In an Ultrex medium mixing bowl stir together flour, oat bran, sugar, baking soda, baking powder and cinnamon. Add egg substitute or beaten egg whites, buttermilk, oil and vanilla; stir to blend. Fold in raisins. Pour about 1/4 cup batter for each pancake. Cook 2 to 3 minutes until bubbles appear and edges look dry. Turn and cook other side 2 to 3 minutes until browned. Makes 18 (3-inch) pancakes.

Variation
Substitute chopped dates or mixed dried fruit for raisins.

Each pancake contains:	**Cal**	**Prot**	**Carb**	**Fib**	**Tot. Fat**	**Sat. Fat**	**Chol**	**Sodium**
	66	3g	11g	1g	2g	0	1mg	118mg

Strawberry Pancakes

These pretty pink pancakes are best when topped with fresh strawberries and powdered sugar.

1 cup all-purpose flour
1/2 teaspoon baking soda
1 teaspoon baking powder
1 cup nonfat strawberry yogurt
2 egg whites
1/3 cup skim milk
1 cup sliced strawberries
Powdered sugar

Preheat griddle. In an Ultrex medium mixing bowl stir together flour, baking soda and baking powder. Beat in yogurt, egg whites and skim milk. Spray griddle with vegetable cooking spray. Pour 1/4 cup batter for each pancake. Cook 2 to 3 minutes until bubbles appear and surface looks dry. Turn and cook other side 2 to 3 minutes until lightly browned. Top cooked pancakes with sliced strawberries. Sprinkle with powdered sugar. Makes 12 (3-inch) pancakes.

				Tot.	Sat.		
Each pancake contains:	**Cal**	**Prot**	**Carb**	**Fib**	**Fat**	**Fat**	**Chol**	**Sodium**
	67	3g	13g	1g	0	0	1mg	85mg

Walnut Sweet-Potato Pancakes

Your guests will never guess the unusual ingredients.

1 cup all-purpose flour
2 tablespoons brown sugar
1/2 teaspoon baking soda
1 teaspoon baking powder
1 cup lowfat buttermilk
2 tablespoons canola oil
2 egg whites
1 teaspoon vanilla extract
1/2 cup mashed, cooked sweet potatoes
1/2 teaspoon pumpkin-pie spice
1/4 cup chopped walnuts

Preheat a non-stick griddle or electric fry pan. In a blender or food processor stir flour, brown sugar, baking soda and baking powder together. Add buttermilk, oil, egg whites, vanilla, sweet potatoes, pumpkin-pie spice and combine. Fold in walnuts. Spray griddle with vegetable cooking spray. Pour about 1/4 cup batter for each pancake. Cook 2 to 3 minutes until bubbles appear and edges look dry. Turn and cook other side 2 to 3 minutes until browned. Makes 15 (3-inch) pancakes.

Each pancake contains:	Cal	Prot	Carb	Fib	Tot. Fat	Sat. Fat	Chol	Sodium
	79	2g	10g	0	3g	0	1mg	75mg

Chocolate Pecan Waffles

Top with fresh sliced fruit or Apricot Sauce, page 207.

1 cup all-purpose flour
2 tablespoons cocoa
1 teaspoon baking powder
1 tablespoon sugar
3 tablespoons pecans
1 cup lowfat cottage cheese
3 tablespoons canola oil
3 egg whites, beaten

Preheat waffle maker. In an Ultrex medium mixing bowl stir together flour, cocoa, baking powder, sugar and pecans. Beat in cottage cheese and oil. Fold in beaten egg whites. Bake according to manufacturer's instructions. Makes about 6 (6-inch) waffles.

Each waffle contains:	Cal	Prot	Carb	Fib	Tot. Fat	Sat. Fat	Chol	Sodium
	217	10g	21g	1g	11g	1g	3mg	236mg

Blue Corn Muffins

Blue cornmeal adds a distinctive flavor and color to these muffins.

2/3 cup blue cornmeal
1-1/3 cups all-purpose flour
1/3 cup sugar
1 tablespoon baking powder
1/4 cup sunflower seeds
2 egg whites, slightly beaten
1/3 cup canola oil
1/2 cup nonfat milk

Preheat oven to 400F (205C). Spray a muffin pan with vegetable cooking spray. In an Ultrex medium mixing bowl stir together cornmeal, flour, sugar, baking powder and sunflower seeds. Make a well in center of mixture and pour in egg whites, oil and milk. Stir until dry ingredients are combined. Spoon batter into prepared muffin pan. Bake about 25 minutes or until a wooden pick inserted into center of a muffin comes out clean.

Remove from pan; cool 5 minutes and serve. Makes 12 muffins.

Each muffin contains:	**Cal**	**Prot**	**Carb**	**Fib**	**Tot. Fat**	**Sat. Fat**	**Chol**	**Sodium**
	177	4g	23g	1g	8g	1g	0	97mg

No-Fuss Fig Muffins

Ready to enjoy in minutes.

2 cups buttermilk baking mix
1/2 cup chopped figs
1/4 cup raisins
1/2 cup packed brown sugar
3 tablespoons canola oil
3/4 cup nonfat milk
1/2 teaspoon almond extract
2 egg whites, beaten

Preheat oven to 400F (205C). Line muffin pan cups with paper baking cups or spray with vegetable cooking spray; set aside. In an Ultrex medium mixing bowl combine baking mix, figs, raisins and sugar. Make a well in center, pour in oil, milk and almond extract. Gently fold together. Batter will be lumpy. Fold in beaten egg whites. Spoon into prepared muffin cups. Bake 17 to 20 minutes or until a wooden pick inserted into center of a muffin comes out clean. Remove from pan; cool 5 minutes and serve. Makes 12 muffins.

Each muffin contains:	Cal	Prot	Carb	Fib	Tot. Fat	Sat. Fat	Chol	Sodium
	188	3g	29g	1g	7g	1g	0	284mg

Orange-Pecan Muffins

A golden-orange interior awaits you.

1-1/2 cups all-purpose flour
1/2 cup rice bran
1 tablespoon baking powder
1/3 cup sugar
1-1/2 teaspoons baking soda
1/4 cup chopped pecans
3 tablespoons canola oil
1 teaspoon vanilla extract
3/4 cup orange juice
1 tablespoon grated orange peel
2 egg whites, beaten

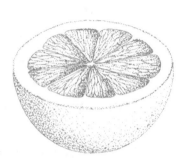

Preheat oven to 400F (205C). Line muffin pan cups with paper baking cups or spray with vegetable cooking spray; set aside. In an Ultrex medium mixing bowl stir together flour, bran, baking powder, sugar, baking soda and pecans. In a cup combine oil, vanilla, orange juice and peel. Stir quickly into flour mixture. Fold in beaten egg whites. Spoon into prepared muffin cups. Bake 17 to 20 minutes or until a wooden pick inserted into center of a muffin comes out clean. Remove from pan; cool 5 minutes and serve. Makes 12 muffins.

	Cal	Prot	Carb	Fib	Tot. Fat	Sat. Fat	Chol	Sodium
Each muffin contains:	147	3g	22g	2g	6g	1g	0	195mg

Prune-Bran Muffins

Start your day with fiber-rich, good-tasting muffins.

1/4 cup egg substitute
1 cup lowfat buttermilk
1/3 cup maple syrup
3 tablespoons canola oil
2 cups unprocessed bran
2/3 cup rice bran
1 tablespoon baking powder
1/2 teaspoon ground allspice
1 cup chopped prunes

Preheat oven to 400F (205C). Spray muffin cups with vegetable cooking spray or line with paper baking cups. In an Ultrex medium mixing bowl combine egg substitute, buttermilk, maple syrup and oil. Add remaining ingredients. Gently fold together until mixture is moistened; batter will be lumpy. Spoon batter into prepared muffin cups. Bake about 20 minutes or until a wooden pick inserted into center of a muffin comes out clean.

Remove from pan; cool 5 minutes and serve. Makes 12 muffins.

Each muffin contains:	<u>Cal</u>	<u>Prot</u>	<u>Carb</u>	<u>Fib</u>	Tot. <u>Fat</u>	Sat. <u>Fat</u>	<u>Chol</u>	<u>Sodium</u>
	125	4g	22g	5g	5g	1g	1mg	116mg

Cornmeal Rolls

Warm rolls provide that special touch to any meal.

1/2 cup cornmeal
1-1/2 cups all-purpose flour
1/2 teaspoon salt
2 tablespoons sugar
2 teaspoons baking powder
1/2 teaspoon baking soda
1/4 cup egg substitute
3/4 cup plain lowfat yogurt

Preheat oven to 425F (220C). In an Ultrex medium mixing bowl combine cornmeal, flour, salt, sugar, baking powder and baking soda. Add egg substitute and yogurt. Stir together, making a soft dough. Roll out to 1/4 inch. Cut in 2-inch rounds. Fold in half. Bake on ungreased baking sheet 15 minutes or until lightly browned. Makes about 24 rolls.

Each roll contains:	Cal	Prot	Carb	Fib	Tot. Fat	Sat. Fat	Chol	Sodium
	50	2g	10g	0	0	0	0	99mg

Lemon-Poppy-Seed Biscuits

Light lemon flavor is a welcome change from the ordinary. If you don't have lemon peel, add 1/2 teaspoon lemon extract.

2 cups all-purpose flour
1 teaspoon grated lemon peel
1 tablespoon baking powder
1-1/2 teaspoons baking soda
1 tablespoon poppy seeds
1 tablespoon sugar
1 cup lowfat lemon-flavored yogurt
1/4 cup nonfat milk
2 tablespoons canola oil

Preheat oven to 450F (230C). In an Ultrex medium mixing bowl stir together flour, lemon peel, baking powder, baking soda, poppy seeds and sugar. Combine yogurt, milk and oil. Make a well in center; add yogurt mixture and stir to blend. Turn out onto a lightly floured surface and gently knead 8 to 10 times. Pat dough to 1/2-inch thickness. With a 2-inch biscuit cutter, cut into 12 to 14 biscuits. Or cut into 2-inch squares. Place on ungreased baking sheet. Bake 10 to 12 minutes or until browned. Makes 12 to 14 biscuits.

Each biscuit contains:	Cal	Prot	Carb	Fib	Tot. Fat	Sat. Fat	Chol	Sodium
	109	3g	18g	1g	3g	0	1mg	170mg

Date-Pistachio Bread

Rich and chewy! Spread slices with Yogurt Cream Cheese, page 1.

1 cup pitted dates, chopped
1/2 cup white grape juice
2/3 cup sugar
1 tablespoon baking powder
1-1/2 cups all-purpose flour
1/2 cup rolled oats
1/2 cup chopped pistachios
1/4 cup canola oil
1/2 teaspoon almond extract
1/4 cup egg substitute or 2 egg whites, beaten

Preheat oven to 350F (175C). Grease a 9 x 5-inch loaf pan; set aside. In an Ultrex medium mixing bowl, soak dates in grape juice about 5 minutes. Stir in sugar, baking powder, flour, rolled oats, pistachios, oil, almond extract and egg substitute or egg whites. Mix until thoroughly combined. Spoon batter into prepared loaf pan and bake 45 to 50 minutes or until a wooden pick inserted in center comes out clean. Cool in pan 10 minutes; turn out on cooling rack. Makes 1 loaf.

Each slice contains:	Cal	Prot	Carb	Fib	Tot. Fat	Sat. Fat	Chol	Sodium
	236	4g	39g	3g	8g	1g	0	95mg

Mango Bread

A wonderful accompaniment to fruit salad.

1-1/2 cups all-purpose flour
1 teaspoon ground cinnamon
1 teaspoon baking soda
1-1/2 teaspoons baking powder
1/4 teaspoon salt
3/4 cup sugar
2 eggs
1/3 cup nonfat milk
3 tablespoons canola oil
1 ripe mango, peeled and chopped
2 tablespoons lemon juice

Preheat oven to 350F (175C). Grease a 9 x 5-inch loaf pan; set aside. In an Ultrex large mixing bowl combine flour, cinnamon, baking soda, baking powder, salt and sugar. In a medium bowl beat eggs slightly; add milk, oil, mango and lemon juice. Stir into dry ingredients until blended. Pour into prepared pan. Bake in preheated oven about 45 minutes or until a wooden pick inserted in center comes out clean. Cool in pan 10 minutes; turn out on cooling rack. Makes 1 loaf.

Each slice contains:	Cal	Prot	Carb	Fib	Tot. Fat	Sat. Fat	Chol	Sodium
	163	3g	28g	1g	4g	1g	36mg	169mg

Carrot-Raisin Loaf

Lemon yogurt combines with carrots for a healthful, yet appetizing bread.

1 cup whole-wheat flour
1 cup all-purpose flour
1 teaspoon baking soda
2 teaspoons baking powder
1/2 teaspoon salt
1/4 teaspoon ground nutmeg
1/2 teaspoon ground cinnamon
2 eggs, beaten slightly
1/3 cup honey
1 cup lowfat lemon yogurt
2 tablespoons canola oil
1/2 cup shredded carrots
1/2 cup chopped raisins

Preheat oven to 325F (165C). Grease a 9 x 5-inch loaf pan; set aside. In an Ultrex large mixing bowl stir together whole-wheat flour, all-purpose flour, soda, baking powder, salt, nutmeg and cinnamon. In a medium bowl combine eggs, honey, yogurt and oil. Add to dry mixture. Stir until well blended. Stir in carrots and raisins. Bake in preheated oven 45 to 50 minutes or until a wooden pick inserted in center comes out clean. Cool in pan 10 minutes. Turn out on cooling rack. Makes 1 loaf.

Each slice contains:	Cal	Prot	Carb	Fib	Tot. Fat	Sat. Fat	Chol	Sodium
	173	5g	32g	2g	4g	1g	36mg	236mg

Prune-Banana Bread

Prunes add extra flavor and moisture to banana bread.

1/3 cup margarine
1 cup sugar
1/2 cup egg substitute or 4 egg whites
1 cup mashed bananas
1-2/3 cup all-purpose flour
1/3 cup oat bran
1 teaspoon baking soda
1 teaspoon vanilla extract
1/2 cup chopped, pitted prunes

Preheat oven to 350F (175C). Grease a 9 x 5-inch loaf pan; set aside. In a mixer bowl beat together margarine and sugar. Beat in egg substitute or egg whites and mashed bananas. Gradually mix in flour, oat bran and baking soda. Stir in vanilla extract and prunes. Spoon batter into prepared loaf pan. Bake about 1 hour or until a wooden pick inserted in center comes out clean. Let cool 10 minutes before removing from pan. Cool before slicing. Makes 1 loaf.

Each slice contains:	Cal	Prot	Carb	Fib	Tot. Fat	Sat. Fat	Chol	Sodium
	202	4g	39g	2g	5g	1g	0	152mg

Oatmeal Herb Yeast Bread

Toast slices for the best tasting sandwiches you've ever eaten.

1/4 cup olive oil
2 tablespoons brown sugar
1 cup warm milk
1/2 teaspoon salt
1/2 teaspoon dried-leaf basil
1/2 teaspoon caraway seeds
1/2 teaspoon dried-leaf tarragon
1 (1/4-oz.) pkg. dry yeast
1-1/2 cup rolled oats
2-1/2 cups all-purpose flour

In a mixer bowl combine oil, brown sugar, milk, salt, basil, caraway seeds, tarragon leaves and yeast. Let stand about 5 minutes. With mixer running, blend in oats and one-half flour. Turn dough out on lightly floured surface and knead in remaining flour. Place dough in a lightly oiled bowl, cover and let rise until double in bulk. Turn dough out, punch down and form in loaf; preheat oven to 375F (190C). Place in a greased 9 x 5-inch pan. Bake 35 to 40 minutes until golden brown and loaf sounds hollow when tapped. Remove from pan and cool. Makes 1 loaf.

Each slice contains:	Cal	Prot	Carb	Fib	Tot. Fat	Sat. Fat	Chol	Sodium
	191	5g	30g	2g	5g	1g	0	102mg

Honey Sunflower Bread

Homemade bread combines goodness and flavor.

1/3 cup honey
2 cups hot water
2 tablespoons margarine
2 tablespoons sunflower seeds
1 cup rolled oats
1 (1/4-oz.) pkg. active dry yeast
1/4 cup warm water
4-1/2 to 5 cups all-purpose flour

In a mixer bowl stir together honey, hot water, margarine and sunflower seeds. Stir in oats. Set aside for 15 to 20 minutes. In a cup stir yeast in warm water, let stand 5 minutes; add to oat mixture. Use a dough hook to beat in about 4 cups flour. Mix thoroughly. Turn out on a lightly floured board. Gently knead adding more flour as necessary. Place dough in a large oiled bowl, turning dough to coat top. Cover; let rise about 1-1/2 hours until doubled in bulk. Punch down dough. Shape into 2 loaves. Place in two greased 9 x 5-inch pans. Let rise again. Preheat oven to 375F (190C). Bake about 50 minutes until loaves sound hollow when tapped. Remove from pan and cool. Makes 2 loaves.

Each slice contains:	Cal	Prot	Carb	Fib	Tot. Fat	Sat. Fat	Chol	Sodium
	124	3g	24g	1g	2g	0	0	13mg

Basic Pizza Dough

Use your favorite topping, or try our Tomato-Onion Topping, page 88.

1 (1/4-oz.) pkg. active dry yeast
1 cup warm water
1 tablespoon olive oil
1/2 teaspoon salt
2 teaspoons finely chopped onion
3 cups all-purpose flour

In a mixer bowl dissolve yeast in warm water. Add oil, salt, chopped onion and 1-1/2 cups flour. Beat until thoroughly combined, making a soft dough. Turn dough out onto a floured surface. Knead in enough flour to make a stiff dough. Spray a bowl with olive oil cooking spray. Place dough in bowl, cover and let rise until doubled in bulk. Punch down dough; cut in half and roll out to fit two 12-inch pans. Makes 2 (12-inch) pizzas.

Each 2-inch slice contains:	Cal	Prot	Carb	Fib	Tot. Fat	Sat. Fat	Chol	Sodium
	125	3g	24g	1g	1g	0	0	90mg

Tomato-Onion Topping

Pizza is great without the cheese, or use this topping on toasted French bread or English muffins.

Basic Pizza Dough, page 87
1 tablespoon olive oil
2 onions, sliced
3 tomatoes, thinly sliced
1/4 cup sliced black olives
Basil to taste
Oregano to taste
Pepper to taste
1 tablespoon olive oil

Prepare Pizza Dough. Preheat oven to 425F (220C). In an Ultrex 10-inch nonstick fry pan heat olive oil. Add onions and sauté briefly. Arrange onion slices on top of pizza dough. Top with sliced tomatoes and olives. Sprinkle with basil, oregano and pepper to taste. Drizzle with olive oil. Bake 15 to 20 minutes until browned. Makes topping for two (12-inch) pizzas.

Topping for each 2-inch slice contains:	Cal	Prot	Carb	Fib	Tot. Fat	Sat. Fat	Chol	Sodium
	18	0	2g	0	1g	0	0	12mg

Beans, Rice & Pasta

Nutritionists are encouraging us to increase our grain consumption. Grains provide vitamins, minerals, protein and fiber needed to maintain a balanced diet.

Before preparing beans, rinse them in water and remove any debris or broken beans. Presoak beans to shorten cooking time. There are two basic methods of presoaking. The first is to place the beans in a large bowl or pan that will accommodate at least double the amount of beans. Pour water to cover beans about 2 to 3 inches, keep covered and soak 8 hours. Or place beans in a pot and cover with water; bring to a boil and cook 2 minutes in rapidly boiling water. Cover, remove from heat and let stand about 1 hour. Drain water and replace with fresh water. Proceed to cook. When using canned beans, rinse with water and drain, thus reducing the sodium.

It is easy to work grains into your diet with just a little thought. Try Golden Rice, Confetti Grits or Barley Skillet Dinner. For a change try some of the less-familiar grains like millet and quinoa. These have been eaten for centuries by people in other countries.

Pasta is climbing to the top of preferred foods. We're told Marco Polo brought pasta from China to Italy. I for one will always be grateful! It's versatile as well as nutritious and combines easily with other foods. It's delicious served hot or cold. Pasta made from semolina is still the most popular. However for variety, try other flavors like spinach, beet, carrot, tomato and whole wheat.

Making your own pasta is easy, especially with the wonderful pasta machines that roll and cut the dough for you. Fresh pasta, unlike dried, cooks very quickly. Overcooking will result in a gummy mess.

Fruited Brown Rice

Dried and fresh fruits combine nicely with the nutty flavor of brown rice.

2 cups cooked brown rice
2 tablespoons toasted almonds
4 dried figs, chopped
1 celery stalk, chopped
1 cup seedless red grapes
1/2 cup lowfat orange yogurt
1/4 cup orange juice
**1 orange, chopped, peeled, or 1 (11-oz.) can
    mandarin oranges, drained**
1 tablespoon fresh mint, if desired

In a large bowl toss together rice, almonds, figs, celery and grapes. In a cup stir together orange yogurt and orange juice. Pour over rice mixture and stir to combine. Garnish with chopped oranges and fresh mint if desired. Cover and refrigerate until chilled. Makes 6 servings.

Each serving contains:	Cal	Prot	Carb	Fib	Tot. Fat	Sat. Fat	Chol	Sodium
	165	4g	34g	4g	2g	0	1mg	22mg

Golden Rice

Delicious as a side dish. Try it with a dollop of Green-Chile Mayonnaise, page 57, or plain yogurt.

2 cups chicken broth
1 cup uncooked long-grain white rice
3/4 teaspoon turmeric
2 green onions, chopped
1/4 cup chopped pistachios
1 (11-oz.) can mandarin oranges, drained

In an Ultrex 2-quart nonstick fry pan bring chicken broth to a boil. Stir in rice and turmeric. Cover and reduce heat to simmer. Cook about 20 minutes. Stir in green onions, pistachios and mandarin orange segments. Gently toss with a fork to combine. Serve hot or cold. Makes 6 servings.

Each serving contains:	Cal	Prot	Carb	Fib	Tot. Fat	Sat. Fat	Chol	Sodium
	189	5g	35g	2g	3g	1g	0	5mg

Mexican Rice

¡Olé! Serve with Soft Chicken Tacos, page 176.

1 cup uncooked long-grain white rice
3/4 cup chopped green bell pepper
1 cup chopped onion
1/4 cup diced celery
2 tablespoons chopped mild green chiles
1 garlic clove, minced
2 tomatoes, peeled, chopped
1/4 cup frozen peas
2 cups chicken broth
1/2 teaspoon dried-leaf oregano
1/2 teaspoon black pepper
1/2 teaspoon chili powder

Spray an Ultrex 12-inch nonstick sauté pan with olive oil vegetable cooking spray; heat over medium heat. Add rice and sauté briefly; do not brown. Remove rice to bowl. In the same skillet sauté green peppers, onion, celery, chiles and garlic until onion is golden brown. Add tomatoes and peas. Return rice to skillet. Add chicken broth to rice along with black pepper, oregano and chili powder. Cover, reduce heat to low and simmer 20 to 25 minutes or until broth is absorbed. Fluff mixture with a fork before serving. Makes 4 servings.

Each serving contains:	Cal	Prot	Carb	Fib	Tot. Fat	Sat. Fat	Chol	Sodium
	235	8g	48g	3g	1g	0	1mg	30mg

Pilaf

Currants and pine nuts add extra crunch to a traditional side dish.

2 teaspoons olive oil
1 onion, chopped
1/4 cup dried currants or chopped raisins
1/4 cup pine nuts
1/2 teaspoon pumpkin-pie spice
1 cup uncooked rice
1 cup vermicelli, broken in 1-inch pieces
2-1/4 cups chicken broth

Heat oil in an Ultrex 10-inch nonstick sauté pan, sauté onion. Add remaining ingredients. Bring to a boil; reduce heat. Cover and cook about 20 minutes until rice is tender and liquid is absorbed. Fluff mixture with a fork before serving. Makes 6 servings.

Each serving contains:	Cal	Prot	Carb	Fib	Tot. Fat	Sat. Fat	Chol	Sodium
	257	8g	46g	2g	5g	1g	0	4mg

Variation
Pilaf Casserole
Add 1/2 cup chopped carrots and 1 cup cooked chopped chicken.

Barbecued Beans

Serve with Sunshine Salad, page 41, and corn bread for a well-balanced meal.

1/4 lb. Canadian bacon, cubed
1 onion, chopped
1-1/2 teaspoons dry mustard
1 cup coffee
1/4 cup lemon juice or vinegar
1/4 cup tomato paste
3/4 cup water
1/2 teaspoon paprika
1/2 teaspoon chili powder
1/2 cup packed brown sugar
2 cups cooked small white beans

Spray an Ultrex 8-inch nonstick fry pan with vegetable cooking spray. Sauté bacon and onion. Pour all ingredients in a 2-quart baking dish or bean pot. Stir to combine ingredients. Bake uncovered in 350F (175C) oven about 1 hour. Makes 8 (1-cup) servings.

Each serving contains:	Cal	Prot	Carb	Fib	Tot. Fat	Sat. Fat	Chol	Sodium
	154	8g	29g	4g	1g	0	7mg	214mg

Boston Beans

Aunt Helen claims this to be the best of the baked beans.

1 lb. navy or small white beans
1-1/2 cups packed brown sugar
1/2 cup molasses
1 large onion, chopped
1/2 cup catsup
1 tablespoon Worcestershire sauce
1 tablespoon maple syrup
1 teaspoon dry mustard
Salt and pepper to taste

Rinse beans, place in an Ultrex 5-1/2-quart nonstick saucepan and cover with water. Bring to a boil, reduce heat; cover and simmer about 1-1/2 hours. Add more water as needed to keep beans covered. Drain beans. Discard liquid. Place beans in a 3-quart casserole or bean pot; add remaining ingredients and stir. Bake at 300F (150C) about 2 hours. If needed, add hot water to keep beans covered. Makes 8 servings.

Each serving contains:	Cal	Prot	Carb	Fib	Tot. Fat	Sat. Fat	Chol	Sodium
	309	6g	74g	6g	0	0	0	291mg

Lima Bake

*A hearty winter meal. Serve with a crusty French bread
and Confetti Salad, page 35.*

**2 cups large dried lima beans
1 cup packed brown sugar
2/3 cup molasses
2 tablespoons horseradish
1/4 lb. Canadian bacon, cubed
Salt and pepper to taste**

Rinse beans. Place in an Ultrex 5-1/2-quart nonstick saucepan
or dutch oven; cover with water. Bring to a boil and cook
2 minutes. Cover and remove from heat. Set aside about
1 hour. Drain liquid and add fresh water to cover by 3 inches.
Bring to a boil; reduce heat and simmer until tender about
1 to 1-1/2 hours. Add more water if necessary to keep beans
covered. In a 2-quart casserole combine beans with
remaining ingredients. Bake in 325F (165C) oven about
1 hour until tender. Season to taste with salt and pepper.
Makes 8 servings.

Each serving contains:	Cal	Prot	Carb	Fib	Tot. Fat	Sat. Fat	Chol	Sodium
	334	13g	70g	14g	1g	0	7mg	226mg

Stove-Top Beans

Ready in minutes to accompany grilled chicken.

2 (16-oz.) cans small white or pinto beans, drained
1 teaspoon canola oil
1 garlic clove, minced
1/4 onion, chopped
1 teaspoon dry mustard
1 (8-oz.) can pineapple chunks in unsweetened
juice

Rinse beans and drain again. Set aside. Heat oil in an Ultrex
3-quart nonstick saucepan. Sauté garlic and onion. Add
remaining ingredients, simmer about 10 minutes. Makes
4 servings.

Each serving contains:	**Cal**	**Prot**	**Carb**	**Fib**	**Tot. Fat**	**Sat. Fat**	**Chol**	**Sodium**
	370	21g	69g	19g	3g	0	0	6mg

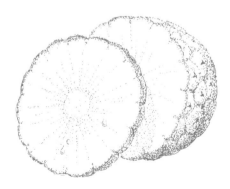

White Bean & Wine Bake

Serve this unusual bean dish with Chicken in Salsa Verde, page 175.

4 cups cooked white beans, drained
1 onion, sliced
1 cup chicken broth
1 cup white wine
1/2 teaspoon chile-pepper flakes
1 tablespoon chopped cilantro (Chinese parsley)
2 tablespoons lemon peel
1/2 teaspoon paprika
Salt and pepper to taste

Preheat oven to 350F (175C). In a baking dish combine all ingredients. Cover and bake 40 minutes. Uncover and bake 15 minutes longer. Makes 4 servings.

Each serving contains:	Cal	Prot	Carb	Fib	Tot. Fat	Sat. Fat	Chol	Sodium
	316	18g	50g	15g	2g	0	0	8mg

Barley Casserole

This will help you cultivate a taste for barley.

2 teaspoons olive oil
1 onion, chopped
2 tablespoons chopped fresh parsley
1 cup sliced mushrooms
1 cup barley
2 cups chicken broth
1/4 cup white wine
1/2 teaspoon thyme
1 teaspoon curry powder
1 (6 oz.) pkg. frozen pea pods, thawed
Salt and pepper to taste

Preheat oven to 350F (175C). Heat oil in a medium baking pan; carefully remove from oven and add onions, parsley, mushrooms and barley. Stir to coat. Add broth, wine, thyme and curry powder. Cover and bake about 45 minutes. Uncover, stir in peas; return to oven 7 to 10 minutes. Makes 8 (1/2-cup) servings.

Each serving contains:	Cal	Prot	Carb	Fib	Tot. Fat	Sat. Fat	Chol	Sodium
	126	5g	21g	6g	2g	0	0	5mg

Barley Skillet Dinner

Because it has a short growing season, barley is grown from the Arctic shores to sub-tropical climates.

1 tablespoon canola oil
1 onion, chopped
2 celery stalks, sliced
2 carrots, sliced
3 cups chicken broth
3 tablespoons lemon juice
3/4 cup quick-cooking barley
1 (10-oz.) pkg. frozen or 3/4 lb. fresh Brussels sprouts
1 cup cubed, cooked chicken
Salt and pepper to taste
2 tablespoons grated Romano cheese

In an Ultrex 12-inch nonstick sauté pan heat oil. Sauté onion, celery and carrots. Add broth and lemon juice; stir in barley. Cover, reduce heat to simmer and cook about 25 minutes. Add Brussels sprouts and chicken. Cover and cook about 10 minutes until sprouts are tender and liquid is absorbed. Season to taste with salt and pepper. Sprinkle with cheese. Serve at once. Makes 6 servings.

Each serving with white meat contains:	Cal	Prot	Carb	Fib	Tot. Fat	Sat. Fat	Chol	Sodium
	150	12g	17g	5g	5g	1g	17mg	70mg

Each serving with dark meat contains:	Cal	Prot	Carb	Fib	Tot. Fat	Sat. Fat	Chol	Sodium
	158	11g	17g	5g	6g	1g	19mg	73mg

Lasagne

Your guests will ask for seconds.

1/2 cup dried mushrooms
1 cup hot water
8 oz. sweet Italian sausage links
1 teaspoon olive oil
1 onion, chopped
2 carrots, sliced
1 celery stalk, sliced
1 (16-oz.) can whole tomatoes
1-1/2 teaspoons Italian seasoning
1 cup dry red wine or tomato juice
1 (8-oz.) pkg. spinach lasagne
1 cup reduced-fat ricotta cheese
1/2 cup nonfat cream cheese
4 oz. mozzarella cheese, thinly sliced
1/4 cup grated Parmesan cheese

Soak mushrooms in hot water about 15 minutes. Remove mushrooms and slice, reserve soaking water. Remove sausage from casing, cook sausage in an Ultrex 3-quart nonstick saucepan until browned, drain excess fat. Add oil and sauté onion, carrots and celery. Add tomatoes, Italian seasoning, wine or tomato juice and reserved mushroom soaking water. Reduce heat and simmer uncovered about 45 minutes. Cook lasagne according to package instructions. Drain and set aside. Spray a 13 x 9-inch baking dish with olive-oil vegetable cooking spray. Combine ricotta and cream cheese. Alternate layers of lasagne, tomato mixture, ricotta mixture and slices of mozzarella. Sprinkle top with Parmesan cheese. Cover and bake at 350F (175C) 30 minutes. Uncover and cook 12 to 15 minutes until top is lightly browned. Makes 15 servings.

Each serving contains:	Cal	Prot	Carb	Fib	Tot. Fat	Sat. Fat	Chol	Sodium
	173	9g	19g	3g	6g	3g	16mg	220mg

Quick & Easy Spaghetti

Amazingly simple; tastes like you've spent hours creating this sauce.

1 lb. sweet Italian sausage links
1/4 onion, chopped
1 (28-oz.) can whole tomatoes, chopped
1-1/2 teaspoons Italian seasoning
1 (8-oz.) can tomato sauce
Cooked spaghetti
Fresh chopped parsley

Slit open and remove casing, and crumble or slice sausage. In an Ultrex 12-inch nonstick sauté pan brown sausages, drain excess fat. Add onion and sauté. Add tomatoes with juice and Italian seasoning. Cover and cook about 20 minutes. Add tomato sauce, cook 5 minutes longer. Serve over spaghetti. Sprinkle with chopped parsley. Makes 6 servings.

Each serving contains:	Cal	Prot	Carb	Fib	Tot. Fat	Sat. Fat	Chol	Sodium
	162	9g	10g	2g	10g	3g	29mg	792mg

Pasta Primavera

Serve warm or chilled. Dinner is ready in 30 minutes.

**1/2 lb. or 1 medium head broccoli, coarsely
  chopped
3 asparagus spears, cut in 2-inch pieces
1 zucchini, halved lengthwise and sliced
1 yellow pepper, sliced
2 garlic cloves, minced
1/4 cup fresh parsley
1/4 cup chicken broth
2 tablespoons dried-leaf basil
1 teaspoon dried-leaf oregano
1 (16-oz.) pkg. pasta
12 cherry tomatoes, halved
Salt and pepper to taste**

Spray an Ultrex 10-inch nonstick fry pan with olive-oil vegetable cooking spray. Add broccoli, asparagus, zucchini, yellow pepper and garlic and sauté 5 to 7 minutes. Set aside. Combine parsley, chicken broth, basil and oregano in blender or food processor. Blend until parsley is fine and moist. Cook pasta in an Ultrex 8-quart multi-cooker according to package directions. Add parsley mixture and tomatoes and toss. Add sautéed vegetables and toss. Season with salt and pepper to taste. Serve warm or chilled. Makes 8 servings.

Each serving contains:	**Cal**	**Prot**	**Carb**	**Fib**	**Tot. Fat**	**Sat. Fat**	**Chol**	**Sodium**
	237	9g	48g	4g	1g	0	0	17mg

Pasta with Vegetable Sauce

Turn the bounty of a garden into a light meal.

1 tablespoon olive oil
1 onion, sliced
2 garlic cloves, minced
1 fennel (sweet anise) bulb, sliced
1 green pepper, sliced
1 red pepper, sliced
1 yellow pepper, sliced
1 cup sliced mushrooms
2 tomatoes, chopped
3/4 cup tomato juice
1/2 teaspoon dried-leaf thyme
1/2 teaspoon dried-leaf basil
1 tablespoon chopped fresh parsley
Cooked macaroni
Grated Parmesan cheese

In an Ultrex 5-1/2-quart nonstick saucepan heat oil. Sauté onion and garlic. Add remaining ingredients. Stir and cook over medium heat until vegetables are tender. Serve over cooked pasta. Sprinkle each serving with grated cheese. Makes 6 servings.

Each serving contains:	Cal	Prot	Carb	Fib	Tot. Fat	Sat. Fat	Chol	Sodium
	58	2g	9g	2g	3g	0	0	128mg

Fettuccine with Herbs and Walnuts

An ideal light lunch or side dish.

1/2 lb. fettuccine
3 tablespoons olive oil
1 tablespoon margarine
1/4 cup minced parsley
2 teaspoons dried-leaf oregano
2 teaspoon dried-leaf basil
1 teaspoon dried-leaf rosemary
2 garlic cloves, minced
3 tablespoons toasted walnuts
2 tablespoons grated Parmesan cheese

Cook fettuccine in an Ultrex 8-quart multi-cooker according to package directions. Cover, set aside. In an Ultrex 8-inch fry pan heat oil, margarine, parsley, oregano, basil, rosemary and garlic. Cook over low heat about 2 minutes. Remove from heat; set aside. In a large serving dish, combine warm fettuccine, herb mixture, walnuts and Parmesan cheese. Toss gently to combine. Serve at once. Makes 4 servings

Each serving contains:	Cal	Prot	Carb	Fib	Tot. Fat	Sat. Fat	Chol	Sodium
	375	10g	45g	3g	17g	3g	2mg	89mg

Zucchini and Pasta in Tomato Sauce

Tender fresh zucchini in a simple sauce.

1 tablespoon olive oil
1/2 large onion, chopped
2 large garlic cloves, minced
1/4 cup chopped Italian parsley
1 teaspoon dried-leaf basil
1/4 teaspoon dried-leaf oregano
1 (28-oz.) can Italian peeled tomatoes
1/4 cup red wine
1/4 cup tomato paste
1/2 cup water
1/2 lb. pasta
1 lb. zucchini, sliced
3 tablespoons grated Parmesan cheese
Salt and pepper to taste

Spray an Ultrex 12-inch nonstick sauté pan with vegetable cooking spray. In prepared skillet heat oil; add onion, garlic, parsley, basil and oregano. Sauté 2 to 3 minutes until onion is soft. Add tomatoes and juice, wine, tomato paste and water. Cover, reduce heat to low and simmer 15 to 20 minutes. Meanwhile, cook pasta in an Ultrex 8-quart multi-cooker according to package directions, omitting salt. Add zucchini to tomato sauce, cover and simmer 10 to 15 minutes or until zucchini is tender. In a large bowl combine tomato sauce and pasta. Sprinkle with cheese and season with salt and pepper to taste. Makes 6 servings.

	Cal	**Prot**	**Carb**	**Fib**	**Tot.** **Fat**	**Sat.** **Fat**	**Chol**	**Sodium**
Each serving contains:	233	9g	40g	5g	4g	1g	2mg	276mg

Zucchini-Stuffed Shells

Jumbo shells provide an interesting way to enhance zucchini for a main dish.

3 medium zucchini, shredded
1/2 teaspoon salt
12 jumbo pasta shells
2 tablespoons canola oil
3 egg whites, beaten slightly
1 tablespoon chopped chives
1/2 cup reduced-fat ricotta cheese
3/4 cup soft bread crumbs
1/8 teaspoon pepper
3/4 teaspoon fines herbs
3 tablespoons margarine
3 tablespoons all-purpose flour
1-1/2 cups nonfat milk
1-1/2 teaspoons chicken bouillon granules
3/4 teaspoon Worcestershire sauce
1/3 cup shredded Monterey Jack cheese

Sprinkle zucchini with 1/2 teaspoon salt; drain in an Ultrex deluxe colander about 15 minutes. Cook pasta in an Ultrex 8-quart multi-cooker according to package directions; drain and toss with oil. With back of spoon, press excess liquid out of zucchini. In an Ultrex medium mixing bowl combine zucchini with egg whites, chives, ricotta, bread crumbs, pepper and fines herbs. Spoon into cooked shells. Place in shallow baking dish. Preheat oven to 350F (175C). In an Ultrex 2-quart nonstick saucepan melt margarine; stir in flour. Cook and stir until mixture is light golden in color. Add milk, bouillon granules and Worcestershire sauce. Cook until thickened. Spoon over filled shells; sprinkle with cheese. Heat about 20 minutes in preheated oven or until bubbly. Makes 12 shells.

				Tot.	Sat.		
Each shell contains:	**Cal**	**Prot**	**Carb**	**Fib**	**Fat**	**Fat**	**Chol**	**Sodium**
	206	8g	27g	2g	7g	2g	6mg	376mg

Confetti Grits

Grits are pleasantly disguised by south-of-the-border flavors.

3 cups chicken broth or stock
1/4 teaspoon salt
3/4 cup quick hominy grits
1 (4-oz.) can diced green chiles, drained
1 medium tomato, peeled, seeded and chopped
1 tablespoon chopped cilantro (Chinese parsley)
1 tablespoon minced green onion
1/4 cup shredded Monterey Jack cheese

Heat chicken stock and salt to boiling in an Ultrex 2-quart nonstick saucepan. Gradually add grits. Cook and stir over medium heat until thickened. Stir in chiles, tomato, cilantro and green onions. Stir in cheese. Makes 6 servings.

Each serving contains:	Cal	Prot	Carb	Fib	Tot. Fat	Sat. Fat	Chol	Sodium
	55	4g	5g	1g	2g	1g	5mg	117mg

Quinoa Casserole

Pronounced KEEN WAH, this nutritious grain is gaining in availability and popularity.

1/2 cup quinoa
1 cup chicken broth
1/4 teaspoon turmeric
1 tablespoon lemon juice
1/2 cup chopped dates
1 cup cubed, cooked chicken
1/2 cup frozen peas
1/4 red or yellow bell pepper, chopped
2 tablespoons chopped dry roasted peanuts

Thoroughly rinse quinoa several times in water. Drain. Pour chicken broth and turmeric into an Ultrex 2-quart nonstick saucepan, add quinoa; bring to a boil. Cover, reduce heat and simmer about 15 minutes until broth is absorbed. Add remaining ingredients and cook until heated. Makes 4 servings.

Each serving with white meat contains:	Cal	Prot	Carb	Fib	Tot. Fat	Sat. Fat	Chol	Sodium
	222	14g	35g	4g	4g	1g	22mg	41mg

Each serving with dark meat contains:	Cal	Prot	Carb	Fib	Tot. Fat	Sat. Fat	Chol	Sodium
	234	12g	35g	4g	6g	1g	25mg	44mg

Lentils with Vegetables

Extra spice adds zest to this hearty dish.

1 cup dried lentils
1/2 onion, chopped
1/2 teaspoon cardamom
1 carrot, sliced
1/2 teaspoon pepper
1 red bell pepper, sliced
1/2 teaspoon ground cinnamon
2 cups water or vegetable stock
1 (16-oz.) can tomatoes
Salt to taste

Rinse and sort lentils. In an Ultrex 3-quart nonstick saucepan combine all ingredients. Bring to a boil. Cover, reduce heat and simmer about 30 minutes until lentils are done. Season to taste with salt. Makes 6 servings.

Each serving contains:	Cal	Prot	Carb	Fib	Tot. Fat	Sat. Fat	Chol	Sodium
	161	11g	29g	6g	1g	0	0	131mg

Vegetables

It is difficult to imagine what our meals would be without vegetables. They provide nutrition, color, texture and flavor. Rapid shipping allows us to enjoy fresh produce from faraway places.

Change from the usual peas and carrots by introducing your family to vegetables that may be less familiar. Try Brussels Sprouts in Mustard Sauce, Leeks with Pepper Sauce, Beets with Raisins or Eggplant Casserole.

An easy way to increase your consumption of vegetables is to simply take your favorite casserole or stir-fry recipe and reduce the meat by half and double the vegetables.

One nice way to prepare all types of vegetables is steaming them. You don't need any special equipment although steamers are very handy. Simply place vegetables of uniform size in a vegetable-steamer basket, strainer or on a rack above a small amount of simmering water. Cover and cook until they are the desired tenderness, adding more water if needed. The water may be seasoned with a tablespoon of lemon juice or wine or by the addition of herbs. Once again be inventive—my recipes are just a guide to get you started in creative cooking. Serve steamed vegetables plain or adorned with seasonings, yogurt or dressing.

I like to serve at least two vegetables of contrasting color and texture with dinner. Think of the dinner plate as a painting: vegetables supply the accents that complete the picture; they please the eye as well as the palate.

Beets with Raisins

A bright vegetable side dish to serve with broiled meat or poultry.

1 (16-oz.) can sliced beets
1/2 cup reserved beet juice
4 teaspoons cornstarch
1/4 cup corn syrup
3 tablespoons lemon juice
1 tablespoon cider vinegar
1 teaspoon lemon peel
1/4 cup chopped onion
1/4 cup raisins

Drain juice from beets, reserving 1/2 cup. Pour reserved beet juice into an Ultrex 2-quart nonstick saucepan with cornstarch, stir until dissolved. Add corn syrup. lemon juice, vinegar, lemon peel and onions. Cook over medium heat until sauce thickens. Add beets and raisins. Pour mixture into a casserole, bake at 350F (175C) about 25 minutes. Makes 4 servings.

Each serving contains:	Cal	Prot	Carb	Fib	Tot. Fat	Sat. Fat	Chol	Sodium
	134	2g	35g	3g	0	0	0	322mg

Brussels Sprouts in Mustard Sauce

A mild mustard sauce adds zest to the Brussels sprouts.

1 (10-oz.) pkg. frozen or 3/4 lb. fresh Brussels sprouts
1/2 cup chicken broth
1 teaspoon canola oil
2 tablespoons chopped green onion
1 cup chicken broth
1 teaspoon Dijon-style mustard
1/2 teaspoon pepper
1 tablespoon cornstarch
1/2 cup evaporated skimmed milk

Cook Brussels sprouts in 1/2 cup chicken broth in an Ultrex 2-quart nonstick saucepan; cover and set aside. Spray an Ultrex 8-inch nonstick fry pan with vegetable cooking spray. Add oil and sauté onion. Remove from heat and slowly add 1 cup chicken broth. Stir in mustard and pepper. Return to heat. Dissolve cornstarch in milk. Pour into mixture. Stirring constantly, cook until sauce is smooth and thickened, about 5 minutes. Pour mustard sauce over cooked Brussels sprouts and stir to coat. Serve at once. Makes 4 servings.

Each serving contains:	Cal	Prot	Carb	Fib	Tot. Fat	Sat. Fat	Chol	Sodium
	94	7g	13g	4g	2g	0	2mg	75mg

Brussels Sprouts with Currants

The addition of currants makes this a special side dish.

1-1/4 cups chicken broth
1 tablespoon chopped onion
2 tablespoons dried currants
1 lb. fresh or 1 (16-oz.) pkg. frozen Brussels sprouts
2 teaspoons cornstarch
1/4 cup water
1/4 teaspoon poultry seasoning
Salt and pepper to taste

Combine chicken broth, onions, currants and Brussel sprouts in an Ultrex 3-quart nonstick saucepan. Cook until Brussels sprouts are tender, about 15 minutes. Remove Brussels sprouts to serving dish, cover and set aside. Dissolve cornstarch in water, add poultry seasoning and stir into cooking liquid. Stir constantly until thickened slightly. Season to taste with salt and pepper. Pour over Brussels sprouts. Serve at once. Makes 6 servings.

Each serving contains:	Cal	Prot	Carb	Fib	Tot. Fat	Sat. Fat	Chol	Sodium
	52	4g	10g	4g	1g	0	0	19mg

Red Cabbage à la Orange

A pretty side dish to serve with Stuffed Pork Tenderloin, page 154.

1 tablespoon canola oil
1 onion, chopped
1 lb. red cabbage, shredded, cored
2 apples, cored, sliced
1/2 cup tomato juice
1/4 teaspoon ground cloves
1 cinnamon stick
1/2 cup red wine
1/2 cup orange marmalade

In an Ultrex 12-inch nonstick sauté pan heat oil. Sauté onion. Stir in cabbage and apples, stir fry until cabbage wilts. Add tomato juice, cloves and cinnamon stick. Cover and simmer about 10 minutes. Add wine and marmalade, mix and cook about 5 minutes longer. Serve hot or cold. Makes 6 servings.

Each serving contains:	Cal	Prot	Carb	Fib	Tot. Fat	Sat. Fat	Chol	Sodium
	165	2g	34g	4g	3g	0	0	90mg

Betty's English Carrots

This is an old family recipe, handed down for generations.

2 cups (4-5) sliced carrots
1 cup small boiling onions
1 cup apple juice
1 firm apple (Granny Smith), sliced in twelfths
1 teaspoon cornstarch
1/4 cup apple juice

In an Ultrex 2-quart nonstick saucepan cook carrots and onions in 1 cup apple juice until tender. Add apple slices and cook until apples are tender. Dissolve cornstarch in 1/4 cup apple juice and add to mixture. Cook and stir about 5 minutes until slightly thickened. Makes 6 servings.

Each serving contains:	Cal	Prot	Carb	Fib	Tot. Fat	Sat. Fat	Chol	Sodium
	77	1g	19g	3g	0	0	0	37mg

Eggplant Casserole

Subtle flavors work well together, serve with Island Slaw, page 39, or a mixed green salad.

1 lb. eggplant, cut in 8 slices
Salt
2 tablespoons canola oil
2 green onions, chopped
2 garlic cloves, minced
4 teaspoons cornstarch
1/2 cup orange juice
1/2 cup chicken broth
1/2 cup evaporated skimmed milk
1/2 teaspoon poultry seasoning
1/4 teaspoon pepper
1 teaspoon orange peel
1 cup sliced mushrooms
1 cup chopped, cooked, skinned chicken breast
2 cups cooked rice
2 tomatoes

Sprinkle eggplant with salt, set aside 30 minutes. Pat with paper towel to remove excess moisture. Brush slices with 1 tablespoon oil and place on a baking sheet. Broil 5 minutes, turn and broil other side. In an Ultrex 8-inch nonstick fry pan heat remaining tablespoon oil and sauté onion and garlic. Dissolve cornstarch in orange juice and chicken broth; stir into onion and garlic. Add milk, poultry seasoning, pepper and orange peel. When mixture has thickened, add mushrooms and chicken. Stir to combine. Spoon rice into a 13 x 9-inch baking dish. Place eggplant slices in one layer over rice. Cut each tomato in 4 thick slices. Top each eggplant slice with a tomato slice. Pour mushroom-chicken sauce over all. Cover with foil and bake 30 minutes in a 350F (175C) oven. Makes 8 servings.

Each serving contains:	Cal	Prot	Carb	Fib	Tot. Fat	Sat. Fat	Chol	Sodium
	168	8g	25g	3g	4g	0	12mg	34mg

Spicy Green Beans

Cauliflower and carrots can be treated in the same manner.

2 lbs. fresh or 2 (10-oz.) pkgs. frozen green beans
1 cup chopped jícama or water chestnuts
2 tablespoons chopped fresh parsley
3 tablespoons chopped pimiento-stuffed olives
1/2 cup Italian Dressing, page 55

Trim ends of fresh green beans. Cook with water to cover in an Ultrex 3-quart nonstick saucepan 10 to 12 minutes, until tender-crisp, drain. If using frozen, cook according to package directions, drain. Combine beans, jícama or water chestnuts, parsley and olives in a shallow bowl. Pour Italian Dressing over bean mixture. Cover and refrigerate at least 2 hours. Stir twice while chilling. Makes 6 servings.

Each serving contains:	Cal	Prot	Carb	Fib	Tot. Fat	Sat. Fat	Chol	Sodium
	98	3g	13g	4g	5g	1g	0	61mg

Leeks with Tarragon-Pepper Sauce

Looks like a giant green onion, but it's sweeter and milder.

8 leeks
1-1/2 cups chicken broth
1 teaspoon dried-leaf tarragon
1/4 cup vermouth or lemon juice
1/2 cup chopped red bell pepper
2 tablespoons cornstarch
1/4 cup skim milk
1 tablespoon chopped chives
Salt and pepper to taste

Trim dark green portion and roots from leeks. Cut in half lengthwise; thoroughly rinse to remove dirt. In an Ultrex 12-inch nonstick sauté pan heat chicken broth, add leeks; cover and simmer 7 to 10 minutes or until tender. Remove leeks to a serving dish; cover and keep warm. Add tarragon and vermouth or lemon juice and bell peppers to broth. Dissolve cornstarch in milk. Stir into broth. Continue stirring until thickened. Add chives. Season to taste with salt and pepper. Pour sauce over leeks. Serve at once. Makes 4 servings.

Each serving contains:	**Cal**	**Prot**	**Carb**	**Fib**	**Tot. Fat**	**Sat. Fat**	**Chol**	**Sodium**
	155	5g	29g	4g	1g	0	1mg	45mg

Mushroom Casserole

Serve with Rosemary-Orange Chicken, page 174.

1 lb. medium mushrooms, whole
1 onion, sliced
2 tomatoes, quartered
1 tablespoon lemon peel
1/2 teaspoon dried-leaf oregano
1/2 teaspoon dill weed
1/2 teaspoon garlic powder
1 tablespoon sunflower seeds

Wipe mushrooms with a damp cloth or paper towel. Trim stems. Spray a baking dish with olive-oil cooking spray. Place mushrooms, onions and tomatoes in prepared dish. Sprinkle with lemon peel, oregano, dill weed, garlic powder and sunflower seeds. Bake uncovered about 20 minutes in a 350F (175C) oven. Serve at once. Makes 4 servings.

Each serving contains:	**Cal**	**Prot**	**Carb**	**Fib**	**Tot. Fat**	**Sat. Fat**	**Chol**	**Sodium**
	68	4g	12g	4g	2g	0	0	11mg

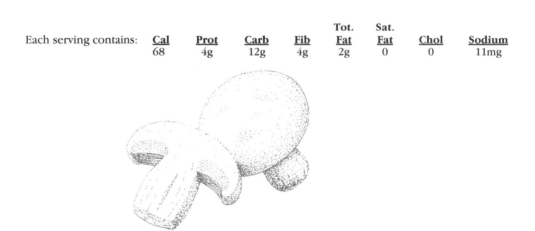

Stuffed Peppers Florentine

When available, use red and yellow bell peppers.

1 (10-oz.) pkg. frozen chopped spinach
1/2 lb. select extra-lean ground beef
1 garlic clove, minced
1 small onion, minced
1/4 teaspoon dried-leaf basil
1/4 teaspoon dried-leaf oregano
2 tablespoons raisins
1/2 cup cooked brown rice
2 tablespoons tomato paste
1 egg white, slightly beaten
4 green bell peppers, seeded, stems removed
2 teaspoons chopped pimiento
2 teaspoons chopped parsley

Preheat oven to 375F (190C). Spray a 8 x 10-inch baking dish with olive-oil vegetable cooking spray. Cook spinach in an Ultrex 2-quart nonstick saucepan according to package instructions. Drain, squeezing out as much liquid as possible. Set aside. Spray an Ultrex 8-inch nonstick fry pan with olive-oil cooking spray. Add beef, garlic and onion. Cook until beef is browned; drain excess fat. In an Ultrex large mixing bowl combine spinach, beef, basil, oregano, raisins, rice, tomato paste and egg white. Fill peppers with mixture and top with pimento and parsley. Place in prepared baking dish. Bake about 30 minutes. Makes 4 servings.

Each serving contains:	**Cal**	**Prot**	**Carb**	**Fib**	**Tot. Fat**	**Sat. Fat**	**Chol**	**Sodium**
	255	19g	22g	4g	11g	4g	49mg	128mg

Potato Sticks

Serve these wedges with Hamburgers Deluxe, page 160, or California Chicken Sandwich, page 184.

2 large baking potatoes, unpeeled
2 tablespoons olive oil
1 teaspoon dried-leaf oregano
1 teaspoon paprika
Salt and pepper to taste

Preheat oven to 425F (220C). Scrub potatoes, pat dry. Cut into eighths. Brush with oil and place in a baking dish. Sprinkle with oregano and paprika. Bake about 35 minutes until potatoes are done. Season to taste with salt and pepper. Makes 4 servings.

Each serving contains:	Cal	Prot	Carb	Fib	Tot. Fat	Sat. Fat	Chol	Sodium
	172	2g	26g	3g	7g	1g	0	8mg

Twice-Baked Potatoes

Make ahead, cover and refrigerate until ready to heat.

3 medium baking potatoes
1/4 cup plain nonfat yogurt
1/2 cup nonfat cottage cheese
1 tablespoon chopped chives
1/4 teaspoon dill weed
1 teaspoon dried-leaf basil
2 teaspoons chopped fresh parsley
1/4 cup grated Parmesan cheese
2 tablespoons chopped pistachios
Paprika

Bake potatoes at 425F (220 C) about 1 hour. Remove from oven and slice in half lengthwise. Carefully scoop out potato pulp, leaving the shell intact. Place shells on a baking sheet.

In an Ultrex large mixing bowl mash potato pulp with yogurt, cottage cheese, chives, dill weed, basil, parsley and 2 tablespoons Parmesan cheese. Fill potato shells, mounding mixture. Sprinkle with remaining cheese, pistachios and paprika. Bake at 375F (190C) 15 to 20 minutes until heated through. Makes 6 servings.

Each serving contains:	Cal	Prot	Carb	Fib	Tot. Fat	Sat. Fat	Chol	Sodium
	159	7g	28g	3g	2g	1g	4mg	149mg

Squash-Cheese Casserole

A colorful medley of vegetables, sure to please most everyone.

2 crookneck squash, sliced
2 pattypan squash, sliced
2 tomatoes, sliced
1 (12-oz.) can cream-style corn, drained
3 green onions, chopped
6 (2/3-oz.) slices lowfat American cheese
2 teaspoons chopped cilantro (Chinese parsley)
1 teaspoon dried-leaf oregano
1 teaspoon dried-leaf marjoram
Salt and pepper to taste

Preheat oven to 350F (175C). Spray a 2-quart casserole with vegetable cooking spray. Combine squash, tomatoes, corn and green onions. Cover and bake 20 minutes. Place cheese slices in one layer over vegetables. Combine cilantro, oregano and marjoram and scatter on top of cheese. Bake uncovered 10 to 12 minutes. Season to taste with salt and pepper. Makes 6 servings.

Each serving contains:	Cal	Prot	Carb	Fib	Tot. Fat	Sat. Fat	Chol	Sodium
	103	2g	16g	3g	3g	0	10mg	447mg

Zucchini-Onion Casserole

If available, use both yellow and green zucchini.

2 tablespoons canola oil
2 cups zucchini slices
1 cup onion slices
1/2 cup sliced mushrooms
2 tablespoons cornstarch
2/3 cup chicken broth
1/4 cup dry sherry
1 teaspoon dill weed
1/2 teaspoon paprika
3 tablespoons bread crumbs
2 tablespoons grated Parmesan cheese

Heat oil in an Ultrex 10-inch nonstick fry pan. Sauté zucchini and onion, stir in mushrooms. Spray a baking dish with vegetable cooking spray. Transfer zucchini mixture to baking dish. In a cup combine cornstarch with chicken broth, sherry, dill weed and paprika. Pour over zucchini. Combine bread crumbs and Parmesan cheese. Sprinkle on top. Bake in 350F (175C) oven about 25 minutes. Makes 4 to 6 servings.

Each serving contains:	Cal	Prot	Carb	Fib	Tot. Fat	Sat. Fat	Chol	Sodium
	91	2g	6g	1g	5g	1g	1mg	42mg

Baked Vegetable Medley

Use fresh vegetables to replace frozen if you prefer.

1 (16-oz.) pkg. frozen mixed vegetables
1 cup beef broth
1/2 teaspoon dried-leaf basil
1/2 teaspoon dried-leaf tarragon
2 teaspoons chopped fresh parsley

Preheat oven to 350F (175C). Combine all ingredients in a shallow baking dish. Bake covered about 15 minutes. Serve hot or cold. Makes 5 servings.

Each serving contains:	**Cal**	**Prot**	**Carb**	**Fib**	**Tot. Fat**	**Sat. Fat**	**Chol**	**Sodium**
	58	3g	12g	4g	0	0	0	32mg

Vegetables with Dill

A colorful medley of favorite vegetables.

1/2 lb. small whole onions, peeled
1 lb. small new potatoes, cubed
6 carrots, peeled and cut into 1-inch pieces
1 cup chicken broth
1 teaspoon dill weed or 2 tablespoons fresh,
**   chopped dill**
1 cup frozen peas

Spray an Ultrex 5-1/2-quart nonstick saucepan with butter-flavor vegetable cooking spray. Sauté onions until lightly browned. Add all remaining ingredients except peas; heat to boiling. Reduce to simmer, cover and cook 30 to 45 minutes, until vegetables are tender. Add peas and cook 5 minutes longer. Makes 6 servings.

Each serving contains:	Cal	Prot	Carb	Fib	Tot. Fat	Sat. Fat	Chol	Sodium
	136	5g	29g	5g	1g	0	0	57mg

Marinated Vegetables

Vary the beans to suit your family's choice. This can be refrigerated several days.

1 (16-oz.) can kidney beans, drained
1 (16-oz.) can lima beans, drained
1 (16-oz.) can black-eyed peas, drained
1 red bell pepper, sliced
1 onion, sliced
1/3 cup sugar
1/2 cup wine or cider vinegar
1/3 cup olive oil
1/2 teaspoon dry mustard
1/2 teaspoon dried-leaf marjoram
1/2 teaspoon dried-leaf basil
2 tablespoons chopped fresh parsley

Rinse drained beans with water and drain again. In a serving bowl combine all ingredients. Cover and marinate at least 6 hours. Serve chilled as a side dish or on lettuce leaves as a salad. Makes 6 to 8 servings.

Each serving contains:	Cal	Prot	Carb	Fib	Tot. Fat	Sat. Fat	Chol	Sodium
	356	12g	51g	18g	13g	2g	0	665mg

Fish & Seafood

The bounty of the sea is waiting for you at your market. Although fresh seafood is preferred, it's not always available. Fortunately, frozen can be a very satisfactory substitute. Modern processing at sea results in very quick freezing, which helps preserve flavor and texture.

If you have a fisherman in the family, encourage him to bring the catch home. To freeze fish at home—slower than commercial freezing—place fish in a shallow pan, fill with water, cover with foil and freeze. After frozen solid, transfer to a plastic freezer bag. Try to include fish in your diet two or three times a week.

Ease of preparation and short cooking time make fish or seafood an ideal choice. Choose to bake, broil, poach, stir-fry or steam your favorite fish. For best results cook fish on high heat for a short time because overcooking both toughens and dries the fish.

And don't overlook the benefits of omega-3—a very, very good fat—gained by eating these foods. Herring, mackerel, salmon, trout and white tuna are some of the best sources of omega-3 fatty acids. However, these benefits can be lost when the fish is deep fried and heavily sauced with butter or cream.

Enjoy the Crab and Pasta if you are in the mood for something cold. Or for a special dish, Orange Roughy in Parchment or Fillets Pacifica vie for the number-one choice. Tender Scallop Kabobs taste so great that no one will suspect it was prepared in minutes. If you are a salmon lover, treat yourself to the Salmon with Curry Sauce.

Baked Fish Pizzaiola

An uncomplicated dish that tastes simply great.

1 lb. flounder fillets
1 garlic clove, minced
1/2 teaspoon dried-leaf basil
Fresh ground black pepper to taste
1-1/2 cups diced fresh tomato
2 green onions, diced
2 tablespoons chopped fresh Italian parsley

Preheat oven to 425F (220C). Spray a baking dish with olive-oil vegetable cooking spray. Place fillets in single layer in baking dish. Spray fillets with olive-oil vegetable cooking spray. Sprinkle minced garlic, basil and pepper over fish. Arrange tomatoes and onions over fish. Sprinkle with parsley. Cover with foil. Bake 10 to 15 minutes or until fish flakes. Makes 4 servings.

Each serving contains:	Cal	Prot	Carb	Fib	Tot. Fat	Sat. Fat	Chol	Sodium
	120	22g	4g	1g	2g	0	54mg	99mg

Baked Catfish Fillets

A crisp coating without frying.

1 lb. skinless catfish fillets
1/2 cup evaporated skimmed milk
1/3 cup cornmeal
1/2 teaspoon paprika
1 teaspoon dill weed
1/4 teaspoon garlic powder

Rinse fillets and pat dry. Set aside. Spray a baking dish with olive-oil vegetable cooking spray. Preheat oven to 425F (220C). Pour milk into a shallow dish or pie plate. Combine cornmeal, paprika, dill weed and garlic in another dish. Dip fillets in milk and then in cornmeal mixture. Place in prepared baking dish. Lightly spray with olive-oil cooking spray. Bake uncovered 10 to 12 minutes or until fish flakes. Makes 4 servings.

Each serving contains:	Cal	Prot	Carb	Fib	Tot. Fat	Sat. Fat	Chol	Sodium
	200	24g	13g	1g	5g	1g	67mg	109mg

Clams in Tomato Sauce

Delicious and easy to prepare in less than 30 minutes.

2 teaspoons olive oil
1 garlic clove
1/4 onion, chopped
1/4 green bell pepper, chopped
2 teaspoons chopped parsley
1/2 teaspoon dried-leaf basil
1 large tomato, chopped, seeded
1/2 teaspoon sugar, if desired
1 (6-oz.) can clams
1/2 cup frozen peas
Cooked pasta
4 teaspoons grated Parmesan cheese

In an Ultrex 10-inch nonstick sauté pan, heat oil, sauté garlic, onion and bell pepper. Stir in parsley, basil, tomato and sugar if desired. Reduce heat, add clams with juice. Cover and simmer 15 minutes. Add peas, cook 5 minutes. Serve over cooked pasta and sprinkle with Parmesan cheese. Makes 4 servings.

Each serving contains:	Cal	Prot	Carb	Fib	Tot. Fat	Sat. Fat	Chol	Sodium
	121	13g	8g	2g	4g	1g	30mg	83mg

Caribbean Cod

Steamed rice and fresh fruit slices complete this meal.

1 lb. poached boneless cod
2 tablespoons olive oil
4 garlic cloves
1/2 onion, sliced
3 tomatoes, chopped
1/4 teaspoon chile-pepper flakes
1 tablespoon capers
2 tablespoons sliced olives
1 tablespoon blanched slivered almonds
2 tablespoons chopped parsley

Cut poached cod into bite-size pieces, set aside. In an Ultrex 12-inch nonstick sauté pan heat oil and garlic cloves. When garlic turns golden, remove from oil and discard. Add onions and sauté. Add tomatoes, chile-pepper flakes and capers. Reduce heat, cover and cook about 15 minutes. Add olives, almonds, parsley and reserved cod. Heat through. Serve at once. Makes 4 servings.

Each serving contains:	**Cal**	**Prot**	**Carb**	**Fib**	**Tot. Fat**	**Sat. Fat**	**Chol**	**Sodium**
	226	27g	8g	2g	10g	1g	62mg	160mg

Cod with Ginger Grapefruit

Mild-flavored cod with a flavorful sauce.

1/4 cup grapefruit juice
1/4 cup orange juice
1 teaspoon grated ginger root
1 teaspoon grated orange peel
1 green onion, chopped
1 garlic clove, minced
1/2 teaspoon sesame oil
1 lb. cod, halibut or orange roughy fillets
1 tomato, sliced
1 grapefruit, segmented

Spray a baking dish with vegetable cooking spray. In an Ultrex small mixing bowl combine grapefruit juice, orange juice, ginger root, orange peel, green onion, garlic and sesame oil. Place cod in baking dish; pour mixture over. Turn cod to coat both sides. Cover and refrigerate about 20 minutes. Remove cover and top cod with tomato slices and grapefruit segments. Spoon sauce over tomatoes. Bake uncovered at 425F (220C) about 10 minutes. Makes 4 servings.

Each serving contains:	Cal	Prot	Carb	Fib	Tot. Fat	Sat. Fat	Chol	Sodium
	138	21g	10g	1g	2g	0	49mg	65mg

Crab and Pasta

Enjoy this as a main dish for lunch or a light supper.

1/2 cup cooked pinto beans, drained
1 (6-oz.) can crab or water-pack tuna
2 green onions, chopped
1 small zucchini, thinly sliced
2 tomatoes, chopped
2 tablespoons chopped sweet pickles
2 cups cooked mostaccioli pasta
1/3 cup Italian Dressing, page 55

Rinse and drain beans. In an Ultrex large mixing bowl combine crab or tuna, beans, green onions, zucchini, tomatoes and pickles. Add hot cooked pasta. Toss all together with Italian Dressing. Serve at once, or cover and refrigerate 2 hours to thoroughly chill. Makes 6 servings.

Each serving contains:	Cal	Prot	Carb	Fib	Tot. Fat	Sat. Fat	Chol	Sodium
	159	10g	21g	3g	4g	1g	25mg	138mg

Fillets Pacifica

Popular flavors borrowed from the Pacific Rim.

1 lb. white fish fillets
1/4 cup low-sodium soy sauce
2 tablespoons lemon juice
1 tablespoon canola oil
1 teaspoon grated fresh
**   ginger root**
1 teaspoon brown sugar
1 green onion, sliced
1 teaspoon toasted sesame seeds

Arrange fish in shallow dish. Combine soy sauce, lemon juice, oil, ginger root, brown sugar and green onion in an Ultrex small mixing bowl. Pour over fish. Cover and refrigerate at least one hour. Drain fish; reserve marinade. Broil fish about 3 inches from heat 3 to 4 minutes on each side. Brush with sauce at least one time. Sprinkle with sesame seeds. Makes 4 servings.

Each serving contains:	Cal	Prot	Carb	Fib	Tot. Fat	Sat. Fat	Chol	Sodium
	154	23g	3g	0	5g	1g	54mg	1125mg

Dilled Halibut Steaks

A bit more flair and flavor than plain broiled fish.

2 tablespoons lemon juice
2 tablespoons celery leaves
1 bay leaf
1 quart water
1 lb. halibut steaks, about 1-inch thick
1/3 cup lowfat plain yogurt
3 tablespoons reduced-calorie mayonnaise
1/2 teaspoon dill weed
2 teaspoons minced chives
1/4 teaspoon salt
1/4 teaspoon pepper
1/4 teaspoon paprika
Lemon wedges

In an Ultrex 12-inch nonstick sauté pan combine lemon juice, celery leaves, bay leaf and water. Bring to a boil. Add halibut steaks; cover and simmer 4 minutes or until barely done. With slotted spoon or spatula, carefully lift fish out of water; place in broiler pan. In a small bowl combine yogurt, mayonnaise, dill weed, chives, salt, pepper and paprika. Spread over top of each steak. Broil 5 or 6 inches from heat source until bubbly and golden on top. Garnish with lemon wedges. Makes 4 servings.

Each serving contains:	**Cal**	**Prot**	**Carb**	**Fib**	Tot. **Fat**	Sat. **Fat**	**Chol**	**Sodium**
	164	25g	4g	0	5g	1g	39mg	265mg

Mahi Mahi Español

Try this delicate-flavored fish from the Pacific.

2 teaspoons olive oil
3 garlic cloves, chopped
1 onion, chopped
4 (1 lb.) tomatoes, chopped
1 green or red bell pepper, chopped, or 1 green
    chile pepper, chopped
3 tablespoons chopped parsley
1/2 teaspoon ground cinnamon
1 lb. mahi mahi, cut in 1-inch cubes
2 tablespoons chopped toasted almonds, sliced

In an Ultrex 10-inch nonstick sauté pan heat oil, sauté garlic and onions. Add tomatoes, peppers or green chiles and parsley. Cook together 3 to 4 minutes. Stir in cinnamon. Add fish cubes, cover and cook 10 minutes. Sprinkle with almonds. Makes 4 servings.

Each serving contains:	Cal	Prot	Carb	Fib	Tot. Fat	Sat. Fat	Chol	Sodium
	191	24g	12g	3g	6g	1g	83mg	114mg

Orange Roughy in Parchment

Make packets of parchment or foil for no-mess baking.

1 carrot, julienned
6 whole Chinese pea pods
2 (6-oz.) orange roughy fillets
1/4 cup lime juice
Paprika
2 tablespoons sliced pimiento-stuffed olives
2 tablespoons capers
2 tablespoons chopped parsley

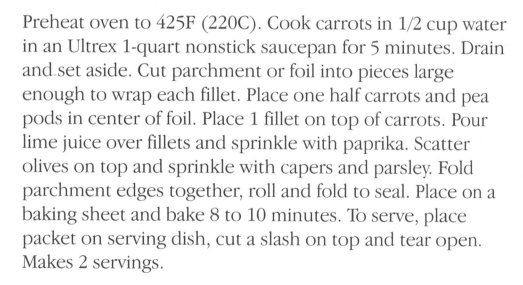

Preheat oven to 425F (220C). Cook carrots in 1/2 cup water in an Ultrex 1-quart nonstick saucepan for 5 minutes. Drain and set aside. Cut parchment or foil into pieces large enough to wrap each fillet. Place one half carrots and pea pods in center of foil. Place 1 fillet on top of carrots. Pour lime juice over fillets and sprinkle with paprika. Scatter olives on top and sprinkle with capers and parsley. Fold parchment edges together, roll and fold to seal. Place on a baking sheet and bake 8 to 10 minutes. To serve, place packet on serving dish, cut a slash on top and tear open. Makes 2 servings.

Each serving contains:	<u>Cal</u>	<u>Prot</u>	<u>Carb</u>	<u>Fib</u>	Tot. <u>Fat</u>	Sat. <u>Fat</u>	<u>Chol</u>	<u>Sodium</u>
	257	26g	9g	2g	13g	0	34mg	293mg

Note: Total fat and saturated fat for orange roughy may be considerably lower due to wax ester content of total lipids.

Red Snapper with Wine Sauce

Raisins and peas add color and interest to a wine sauce.

1 teaspoon olive oil
1 green onion, chopped
1/4 cup red bell pepper, sliced
1 garlic clove, minced
2 tablespoons raisins
1/4 teaspoon ground cinnamon
3/4 cup white wine
1/2 cup frozen petite peas
1 lb. red snapper fillets

Preheat oven to 450F (230C). In an Ultrex 8-inch nonstick fry pan heat oil and sauté green onion, red bell pepper and garlic. Add raisins, cinnamon, wine and peas. Spray a baking dish with vegetable cooking spray. Rinse fillets and pat dry. Place in baking dish. Spoon wine mixture over fillets. Cover and bake 5 minutes; remove cover. Spoon sauce over fish and bake another 5 minutes. Serve with sauce. Makes 4 servings.

Each serving contains:	**Cal**	**Prot**	**Carb**	**Fib**	**Tot. Fat**	**Sat. Fat**	**Chol**	**Sodium**
	187	25g	8g	2g	3g	1g	42mg	96mg

Broiled Red Snapper

A creamy topping with a blush of color.

1/3 cup plain lowfat yogurt
1 tablespoon tomato sauce
1/2 teaspoon paprika
1 tablespoon capers
2 teaspoons fresh chopped parsley
3/4 lb. red snapper fillets

In a cup mix yogurt, tomato sauce, paprika, capers and parsley. Spray a broiling pan with vegetable cooking spray. Place fillets on broiler pan; spread fillet tops with yogurt mixture. Broil without turning 6 to 8 minutes, until done. Makes 4 servings.

Each serving contains:	**Cal**	**Prot**	**Carb**	**Fib**	**Tot. Fat**	**Sat. Fat**	**Chol**	**Sodium**
	98	19g	2g	0	1g	0	32mg	92mg

Salmon with Curry Sauce

A mild curry sauce is a natural for the delicate salmon flavor.

1 lb. salmon fillets
1 teaspoon canola oil

Curry Sauce:
1 tablespoon canola oil
1 tablespoon chopped chives
1 tablespoon curry powder
1 teaspoon dry mustard
1/4 cup white wine
2 tablespoons lemon juice
1 tablespoon dried currants
1 teaspoon cornstarch
3/4 cup evaporated skimmed milk

Spray a broiler pan with vegetable cooking spray. Rinse fillets and pat dry. Brush fillets with 1 teaspoon oil and broil about 10 minutes per inch of fish. In an Ultrex 8-inch nonstick fry pan heat 1 tablespoon oil. Stir in chives, curry powder and mustard. Blend thoroughly. Remove from heat; stirring constantly add wine and lemon juice. Return to heat and add currants. Dissolve cornstarch in milk; stir into curry mixture. Blend. Remove broiled fish to serving dishes and top with curry sauce. Serve at once. Makes 4 servings.

Each serving contains:	Cal	Prot	Carb	Fib	Tot. Fat	Sat. Fat	Chol	Sodium
	263	26g	9g	1g	12g	1g	64mg	107mg

Scallop Kabobs

The delicate flavor of scallops is accented by the Italian Dressing.

1 cup Italian Dressing, page 55
1 lb. scallops
1 small onion, quartered
1 red bell pepper, seeded, cubed
12 small fresh mushrooms
1 green bell pepper
Cooked rice

Pour Italian Dressing into an Ultrex medium mixing bowl. Add scallops and onion, toss to coat all pieces. Cover and refrigerate at least 2 hours. Preheat broiler. Alternate scallops, onion, red pepper, mushroom and green pepper on skewers. Broil, turning often, about 7 minutes. Serve with steamed rice. Makes 4 servings.

Each serving contains:	Cal	Prot	Carb	Fib	Tot. Fat	Sat. Fat	Chol	Sodium
	242	20g	8g	1g	15g	2g	37mg	198mg

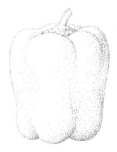

Sea Bass in Salsa

Choose the level of hotness by selecting either the mild Anaheim Chile or the hotter Jalapeño.

1 cup chopped tomatoes
1 cup chopped fresh tomatillos
1/4 onion, chopped
1 mild chile pepper or jalapeño, chopped
1/2 teaspoon dried-leaf oregano
Salt and pepper to taste
1 lb. sea bass fillets

Spray an Ultrex 8-inch nonstick fry pan with olive-oil cooking spray. Add tomatoes, tomatillos and onions. Cook and stir 3 to 5 minutes. Add chile pepper, oregano and salt and pepper to taste. Cook about 5 minutes longer. Preheat oven to 425F (220C). Spray a baking dish with olive oil cooking spray. Rinse fillets and pat dry. Place fillets in a single layer in prepared baking dish. Spoon tomato mixture on top. Cover and bake 10 to 15 minutes or until fish flakes. Serve at once. Makes 4 servings.

Each serving contains:	Cal	Prot	Carb	Fib	Tot. Fat	Sat. Fat	Chol	Sodium
	157	23g	6g	2g	5g	1g	77mg	89mg

Shrimp Broil

Scallops, sea bass or cod can be subsituted for shrimp.

1 (12-oz.) can beer
1/4 teaspoon chile-pepper flakes
1/2 teaspoon dry mustard
1 tablespoon lime juice
2 green onions, chopped
1/4 teaspoon paprika
1/2 to 3/4 lb. shrimp, peeled and deveined, or cod

In an Ultrex medium mixing bowl mix beer, chile flakes, mustard, lime, onions and paprika. Add shrimp or cod, marinate 3 to 4 hours. Spray broiler pan with vegetable spray to prevent shrimp from sticking. Broil at 450F (230C) or high broil 7 to 10 minutes until done. Turn at least once, brush with more marinade if necessary. Serve at once. Makes 4 servings.

Each serving contains:	**Cal**	**Prot**	**Carb**	**Fib**	**Tot. Fat**	**Sat. Fat**	**Chol**	**Sodium**
	98	12g	4g	1g	1g	0	86mg	89mg

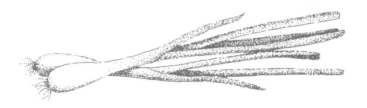

Baked Sole with Carrots and Zucchini

Cook fish on high heat for a short time to keep it moist and flaky.

2 carrots, julienned
1 medium zucchini, julienned
1 lb. sole fillets
Salt and pepper to taste
1 garlic clove, minced
1/2 lemon, thinly sliced
1 tablespoon chopped fresh dill

Preheat oven to 425F (220C). Steam carrots and zucchini in an Ultrex 2-quart nonstick saucepan, using steamer insert, until tender crisp. Spray a baking dish with vegetable cooking spray, add fillets. Season to taste with salt and pepper. Sprinkle with garlic. Arrange lemon slices over fillets. Add vegetables and sprinkle dill over all. Cover loosely and bake in preheated oven 15 minutes or until fish flakes. Makes 4 servings.

Each serving contains:	**Cal**	**Prot**	**Carb**	**Fib**	**Tot. Fat**	**Sat. Fat**	**Chol**	**Sodium**
	126	22g	5g	2g	1g	0	54mg	105mg

Sole Florentine

Mushrooms and pimiento brighten the creamed spinach filling.

2 teaspoons olive oil
1/2 onion, chopped
1 garlic clove, minced
2 tablespoons all-purpose flour
1 cup nonfat milk
1/2 cup sliced mushrooms
2 tablespoons pimiento, chopped
1/4 teaspoon ground nutmeg
1 (10-oz.) pkg. frozen spinach, thawed, drained
1 lb. sole fillets

Preheat oven to 425F (220C). In an Ultrex 2-quart nonstick saucepan heat oil, sauté onion and garlic. Stir in flour and milk. Cook, stirring, until thickened. Stir in mushrooms, pimiento, nutmeg and spinach. Thoroughly combine. Spread mixture on fillets. Roll up and secure with wooden picks, place in a baking dish. Cover and bake about 15 minutes. Makes 4 servings.

Each serving contains:	Cal	Prot	Carb	Fib	Tot. Fat	Sat. Fat	Chol	Sodium
	186	26g	11g	3g	4g	1g	55mg	180mg

Baked White Fish

Select your favorite white fish and cereal coating.

1 lb. white fish fillets
1 tablespoon lime or lemon juice
1 egg white
1/4 teaspoon low-sodium soy sauce
1/3 cup shredded-wheat cereal crumbs
1/3 cup rice bran
1/4 teaspoon five-spice powder

Spray an 8-inch square baking dish with vegetable cooking spray. Preheat oven to 400F (205C). Rinse fish and pat dry. Drizzle lime or lemon juice over fish; set aside. In a pie plate or shallow pan lightly beat egg white and soy sauce. In another pie plate combine shredded wheat crumbs with rice bran and five-spice powder. Dip fillets in egg-white mixture, then into crumb mixture. Place in prepared dish. Bake uncovered about 15 minutes. Serve at once. Makes 4 servings.

Each serving contains:	Cal	Prot	Carb	Fib	Tot. Fat	Sat. Fat	Chol	Sodium
	164	26g	7g	2g	4g	1g	36mg	97mg

Meats

Beef is not bad—just eat less. Make it a habit to trim all visible fat from cuts of beef, pork or lamb. You can easily extend ground-meat dishes by adding 1/2 cup rice or oat bran for each pound of meat. For those who are concerned with the saturated-fat content, choose flank and top-round steaks. For easy slicing, partially freeze flank or top-round steak before attempting to cut it into thin strips. This is especially helpful when preparing stir-fry dishes. Broiled Flank Steak has a mystery ingredient that adds to the flavor.

If you have leftover steak, slice it thinly and refrigerate. Then create your own chef's salad by combining the chilled meat with vegetables and salad greens.

Lamb Kabobs are extra moist, tender and flavorful when marinated in seasoned yogurt. My Corned Leg of Lamb recipe is a variation of one from my friend Beryl Kirby in Sydney, Australia. This dish is as popular there as corned beef is in North America.

I have included pork in my choice of recipes. Because of the new methods of feeding, pork is not as fat as it was 20 years ago. The Stuffed Pork Tenderloin is a delicious entrée for entertaining. You will also find Pacific Rim Stir-Fry a great blend of Oriental flavors. Canadian bacon is also great for seasoning or as a side dish.

Corned Leg of Lamb

Served hot or chilled, an ideal dish for your next party.

4 lb. boneless leg of lamb

Marinade:
2 tablespoons sugar
3 garlic cloves
3 tablespoons pickle spice
1 onion, sliced
1 bay leaf
6 cloves
2 cups apple juice

Trim all visible fat from lamb. Place in an Ultrex large mixing bowl with marinade. Cover. Marinate overnight or up to 3 days. Transfer to Ultrex 5-1/2-quart Saucepan; bring to boil, reduce heat. Cook, simmering until meat is tender, about 2 hours. Drain, discard bay leaf, serve hot or chilled. Makes 10 servings.

Each serving contains:	Cal	Prot	Carb	Fib	Tot. Fat	Sat. Fat	Chol	Sodium
	299	38g	10g	0	11g	5g	122mg	95mg

Marinated Lamb Kabobs

For a more intense flavor, refrigerate lamb in marinade for 2 days before cooking.

1/2 cup plain nonfat yogurt
1/8 teaspoon ground cinnamon
1/8 teaspoon ground cloves
2 teaspoons chopped fresh parsley
1 tablespoon lemon juice
1/2 teaspoon dried onion flakes
1/2 teaspoon fines herbs
1-1/2 lbs. boneless leg of lamb, cubed, trimmed
18 cherry tomatoes
2 green peppers, cut in cubes
1 onion, cut in 16 pieces

In an Ultrex large mixing bowl combine yogurt, cinnamon, cloves, parsley, lemon juice, onion flakes and fines herbs. Add lamb and stir to coat all pieces. Cover and refrigerate 4 hours or overnight. Thread alternate pieces of lamb, tomatoes, green pepper and onion on skewers. Broil, turning several times. Makes 6 servings.

Each serving contains:	Cal	Prot	Carb	Fib	Tot. Fat	Sat. Fat	Chol	Sodium
	214	28g	7g	1g	8g	3g	85mg	82mg

Lamb Patties

For those of you who like lots of spice.

3/4 lb. lean lamb, ground
4 green onions, chopped
1/4 teaspoon garlic powder
1 tablespoon fresh parsley
1/2 teaspoon paprika
1/2 teaspoon dried-leaf oregano
1/2 teaspoon chopped dried-leaf rosemary
1/4 teaspoon cumin
1 egg white
1/4 cup cooked brown rice

In an Ultrex medium mixing bowl thoroughly combine all ingredients. Shape into 4 patties. Broil 7 to 10 minutes on each side. Makes 4 servings.

Each serving contains:	**Cal**	**Prot**	**Carb**	**Fib**	**Tot. Fat**	**Sat. Fat**	**Chol**	**Sodium**
	132	17g	4g	1g	5g	2g	51mg	55mg

Cranberry-Wine Tenderloin

These fruit flavors enhance the tender pork.

1-1/2 lbs. trimmed, boneless pork tenderloin
2 teaspoons canola oil
1 (8-oz.) can whole cranberry sauce
1/4 cup red currant jelly
1/4 cup marsala wine
1 tablespoon lemon juice

Cut pork into 1-inch-thick slices. In an Ultrex 12-inch nonstick sauté pan heat oil and sauté slices. In an Ultrex medium mixing bowl combine remaining ingredients. Remove skillet from heat and slowly add cranberry mixture. Partially cover and cook about 20 minutes, until meat is well done. Makes 6 servings.

Each serving contains:	Cal	Prot	Carb	Fib	Tot. Fat	Sat. Fat	Chol	Sodium
	302	25g	25g	1g	10g	3g	62mg	66mg

Stuffed Pork Tenderloin

Ideal for that special Sunday dinner, served with steamed broccoli and Red Cabbage à la Orange, page 115.

1 teaspoon dry mustard
1/2 teaspoon dried-leaf thyme
1/2 teaspoon paprika
1/2 teaspoon garlic powder
1 teaspoon orange peel
1 lb. trimmed, boneless pork tenderloin
8 to 10 dried apricots
3 tablespoons low-sugar orange marmalade

In a cup stir together mustard, thyme, paprika, garlic powder and orange peel. Lay tenderloin open flat, sprinkle with 3/4 of herb mixture. Place apricots in a row down center of one-half of tenderloin. Lift other half over apricots and secure by tying with string at 2-inch intervals, making a firm roll. Place on a baking rack; sprinkle remaining herbs on top, patting them in. Bake at 350F (175C) about 40 minutes. Spread marmalade over top; continue baking 15 to 20 minutes. Remove from oven, cover with foil and let rest for 10 minutes before slicing. Makes 4 servings

Each serving contains:	Cal	Prot	Carb	Fib	Tot. Fat	Sat. Fat	Chol	Sodium
	255	24g	12g	1g	12g	4g	67mg	43mg

Pacific Rim Stir-Fry

Be sure to trim all the fat off pork before cutting it into strips.

3/4 cup orange juice
1/3 cup dry white wine
1 garlic clove, crushed
2 tablespoons hoisin sauce
1 tablespoon low-sodium soy sauce
1 tablespoon honey
10 oz. boneless lean pork
1 large sweet potato, peeled
2 tablespoons canola oil
1 teaspoon chicken bouillon granules
1 tablespoon cornstarch
4 green onions, cut into 1-inch lengths
1 red bell pepper, halved and sliced
1/4 lb. Chinese pea pods, trimmed
Salt and pepper to taste
3 cups cooked rice
2 nectarines, sliced

In an Ultrex medium mixing bowl combine orange juice, wine, garlic, hoisin sauce, soy sauce and honey. Cut pork into strips about 1/4 x 1/2 x 1-1/2 inches. Add to marinade, cover and refrigerate at least 1 hour. Cut sweet potato into 1/8-inch crosswise slices; halve each slice. Heat oil in an Ultrex stir-fry pan or 12-inch nonstick fry pan. Add sweet potato slices; stir-fry 2 or 3 minutes until softened. Drain pork; reserve marinade. Add bouillon granules and cornstarch to marinade. Add drained pork to pan; cook and stir until meat is no longer pink. Stir in onions, bell pepper and reserved marinade. Cook until slightly thickened. Add pea pods. Sprinkle with salt and pepper to taste. Serve over cooked rice. Arrange sliced nectarines around each serving. Makes 4 servings.

Each serving contains:	**Cal**	**Prot**	**Carb**	**Fib**	**Tot. Fat**	**Sat. Fat**	**Chol**	**Sodium**
	490	23g	67g	3g	13g	3	39mg	884mg

Chinese Steak in Plum Sauce

Hoisin sauce is found in the Oriental food section of your supermarket.

1-1/4 lb. flank steak

Marinade:
2/3 cup plum jam
5 teaspoons hoisin sauce
1 tablespoon lemon juice
2 tablespoons cider vinegar
1/4 teaspoon powdered ginger

Trim any visible fat from steak; cut into quarters. Cut across the grain into thin diagonal strips. In an Ultrex medium mixing bowl combine all marinade ingredients. Add steak strips to marinade, tossing to coat all pieces thoroughly. Cover and refrigerate at least 30 minutes. Remove strips from marinade and thread on skewers. Broil about 2 minutes on each side. Brush with more marinade if needed. If you prefer, stir-fry rather than broil. Makes 6 servings.

Each serving contains:	Cal	Prot	Carb	Fib	Tot. Fat	Sat. Fat	Chol	Sodium
	243	19g	26g	0	7g	3g	47mg	73mg

Broiled Flank Steak

Invite your guests to identify the marinade ingredients.

Marinade:
1 teaspoon instant coffee granules
2 tablespoons hot water
garlic clove
1/2 teaspoon dry mustard
teaspoon dried-leaf tarragon
2 tablespoons olive oil
2 tablespoons vermouth
2 tablespoons lemon juice

1 lb. flank steak, cut in 4 pieces
1 tablespoon cornstarch

Dissolve coffee granules in hot water. Combine remaining marinade ingredients. Place round steak in a shallow baking dish; pour marinade over steak, cover and refrigerate about 3 hours. Spray an Ultrex 12-inch nonstick fry pan with vegetable cooking spray. Heat skillet and pan broil or place on broiler pan and cook as desired. Dissolve cornstarch in marinade; pour into an Ultrex 1-quart nonstick saucepan and heat until thickened. Pour over cooked meat. Makes 4 servings.

Each serving contains:	Cal	Prot	Carb	Fib	Tot. Fat	Sat. Fat	Chol	Sodium
	253	23g	3g	0	15g	5g	57mg	85mg

Stir-Fry Beef with Apricots

For best results, partially freeze steak before slicing into thin strips.

2 tablespoons canola oil
2 garlic cloves
1 tablespoon sliced fresh ginger root
1 lb. lean sirloin steak, thinly sliced
4 green onions, cut in 2-inch pieces
1/2 cup frozen peas
1/2 cup sliced water chestnuts
6 fresh apricots, pitted, sliced in half,
  or 1 (16-oz.) can apricots, drained
2 tablespoons chopped pistachios or walnuts
2 teaspoons cornstarch
2 tablespoons low-sodium soy sauce
2 tablespoons dry sherry
Cooked rice or noodles

Heat oil in an Ultrex stir-fry pan or 12-inch nonstick fry pan. Cook garlic and ginger root until golden; remove and discard. Add steak slices and quickly stir-fry until meat is no longer pink, about 2 minutes. Add onions, peas and water chestnuts. Continue to stir-fry about 1 minute. Add apricots and pistachios or walnuts, stir until heated. In a cup combine cornstarch, soy sauce and sherry; stir to dissolve cornstarch. Pour into stir-fry pan, stirring until slightly thickened and pieces are well coated. Serve over rice or noodles. Makes 4 servings.

Each serving contains:	Cal	Prot	Carb	Fib	Tot. Fat	Sat. Fat	Chol	Sodium
	335	26g	16g	3g	18g	4g	57mg	624mg

Chile Beef and Bean Burgers

Beans provide the extra fiber, chiles the extra flavor.

6 tablespoons cooked pinto beans, drained, mashed
3/4 lb. select extra-lean beef
2 green onions, chopped
1/4 cup chopped green chiles
1-1/2 tablespoons catsup
1 teaspoon dried-leaf oregano
Salt and pepper to taste
4 English muffins, split
Lettuce

In an Ultrex medium mixing bowl, combine all ingredients except English muffins and lettuce. Shape into 4 patties. Heat broiler. Spray broiler pan with vegetable cooking spray. Place patties on prepared broiler pan. Broil 7 to 10 minutes on each side or until cooked through. Toast muffins, top with burger and lettuce. Makes 4 burgers.

					Tot.	Sat.		
Each burger contains:	**Cal**	**Prot**	**Carb**	**Fib**	**Fat**	**Fat**	**Chol**	**Sodium**
	404	27g	33g	4g	17g	7g	74mg	513mg

Hamburgers Deluxe

Juicy patties with wonderful flavor.

2 green onions, chopped
1 teaspoon Dijon-style mustard
1 tablespoon pickle relish
2 tablespoons tomato catsup
1/4 teaspoon garlic powder
3/4 lb. flank steak, ground
1/4 cup oat bran
4 hamburger buns
Lettuce
Alfalfa sprouts, if desired
Salt and pepper to taste

In an Ultrex medium mixing bowl, combine onions, mustard, relish, catsup, garlic powder, beef and oat bran. Thoroughly mix together. Shape into 4 patties. Broil 7 to 10 minutes on each side or until cooked through. Slice hamburger buns in half, lightly toast. Top with meat patty, lettuce and alfalfa sprouts, if desired. Season to taste with salt and pepper. Makes 4 burgers.

Each burger contains:	Cal	Prot	Carb	Fib	Tot. Fat	Sat. Fat	Chol	Sodium
	284	22g	30g	3g	9g	3g	43mg	468mg

Open-Face Roast Pork Sandwich

Accompany this hardy sandwich with Sunshine Salad, page 41.

4 teaspoons Dijon-style mustard
4 slices pumpernickel bread
4 lettuce leaves
4 thinly sliced Stuffed Pork Tenderloin, page 168
12 sliced pickled beets
1 onion slice, separated into rings
Dill weed

Spread mustard on one side of bread slices. Place two slices on each plate. Add a layer of lettuce and pork. Alternate beets and onions on top of pork. Sprinkle with dill weed. Makes 2 servings.

Each serving contains:	Cal	Prot	Carb	Fib	Tot. Fat	Sat. Fat	Chol	Sodium
	150	10g	21g	2g	4g	1g	16mg	293mg

Poultry

My poultry recipes offer you the option of choosing light or dark meat. Removing the skin helps reduce the fat. For those who may not have an elevated cholesterol and prefer dark meat, I've included nutritional information for comparison. Choose whichever meets your needs. You can easily substitute chicken and turkey for other meats in many recipes.

When shopping for poultry, compare the per-pound pricing. Bear in mind that poultry skin and bones account for 60% to 70% of the total weight. Sometimes boned skinned chicken seems higher priced but may actually cost less for the edible portion.

Be guided in your purchase of poultry by the type of cooking you do. If you like to make soups and salads, the whole chicken may be your choice. Bone out the breasts and refrigerate or freeze; cook the remaining for stock. Finally, cool and bone the cooked chicken for salads or sandwiches. Always remember to skin or remove any visible fat. If you are concerned that skinned, boned poultry seems too dry, be careful not to overcook.

I think marinating helps to tenderize as well as keeps poultry moist. Marinades can be as simple as an Italian dressing, barbecue sauce or yogurt. Braising chicken is an easy and fast cooking method. Covering while cooking also helps to seal in moisture. When grilling or barbecuing, turn pieces often to assure even cooking.

Because ovens differ so much, when baking check for doneness about 10 minutes before time suggested in recipe. Boneless, skinless pieces can overcook very easily.

Personalize the recipes as you choose by using different vegetables, fruits or seasonings.

Grilled Chile Chicken

The true taste of the Southwest.

2 tablespoons lemon juice
1/2 teaspoon dried-leaf oregano
1/4 teaspoon paprika
1 lb. chicken pieces, skinned, boned
2 tablespoons canola oil
1/4 cup chopped onion
1 clove garlic, chopped
1 mild green chile, chopped
1 tomato, chopped
3 oz. mozzarella cheese, thinly sliced
1 tablespoon chopped cilantro (Chinese parsley)

Mix lemon juice, oregano and paprika. Pour over chicken; turn pieces, refrigerate 1 hour or more. Heat oil in an Ultrex 8-inch nonstick fry pan, sauté onion and garlic; add chiles and tomatoes. Broil chicken pieces, remove; place cheese on top. Spoon chile mixture on top. Return to broiler, heat until cheese melts. Sprinkle with chopped cilantro. Serve at once. Makes 4 servings.

Each serving with white meat contains:	**Cal**	**Prot**	**Carb**	**Fib**	Tot. **Fat**	Sat. **Fat**	**Chol**	**Sodium**
	263	33g	5g	1g	12g	3g	77mg	189mg

Each serving with dark meat contains:	**Cal**	**Prot**	**Carb**	**Fib**	Tot. **Fat**	Sat. **Fat**	**Chol**	**Sodium**
	274	29g	5g	1g	15g	4g	105mg	213mg

Chicken Cilantro

Complete this meal with Spicy Green Beans, page 118, and warm flour tortillas.

1 lb. chicken pieces, skinned, boned
1/2 teaspoon paprika
2 teaspoons canola oil
2 green onions, chopped
1/4 cup chopped cilantro (Chinese parsley) or parsley
1 tomato, chopped
1/2 cup orange juice

Sprinkle chicken pieces with paprika, patting it in. Heat oil in an Ultrex 10-inch nonstick sauté pan and brown chicken. Add remaining ingredients. Cover, reduce heat, cook about 15 minutes. Turn chicken at least twice during cooking. Makes 4 servings.

Each serving with white meat contains:	**Cal**	**Prot**	**Carb**	**Fib**	**Tot. Fat**	**Sat. Fat**	**Chol**	**Sodium**
	166	27g	5g	1g	4g	1g	65mg	77mg

Each serving with dark meat contains:	**Cal**	**Prot**	**Carb**	**Fib**	**Tot. Fat**	**Sat. Fat**	**Chol**	**Sodium**
	177	23g	5g	1g	7g	1g	94mg	101mg

Chicken with Green Grapes

Yet another way to combine chicken and fruit.

Marinade:
2 tablespoons lemon juice
2 tablespoons cider vinegar
1 tablespoon catsup
2 teaspoons canola oil
1/4 cup white grape juice concentrate
1/4 teaspoon sweet paprika
1/2 teaspoon dry mustard
1 teaspoon dried-leaf basil
1/4 teaspoon onion powder

2 teaspoons canola oil
1 lb. boneless, skinless chicken pieces
1 cup fresh green seedless grapes

Combine marinade ingredients in an Ultrex medium mixing bowl. Add chicken, cover and refrigerate at least 2 hours. Spray an Ultrex 10-inch nonstick sauté pan with vegetable cooking spray. Heat; add oil and chicken pieces, lightly brown. Add marinade, cover and simmer about 15 minutes. Add grapes, cook until heated. Serve at once. Makes 4 servings.

Each serving with white meat contains:					Tot.	Sat.		
	Cal	**Prot**	**Carb**	**Fib**	**Fat**	**Fat**	**Chol**	**Sodium**
	233	27g	18g	1g	6g	1g	65mg	121mg

Each serving with dark meat contains:					Tot.	Sat.		
	Cal	**Prot**	**Carb**	**Fib**	**Fat**	**Fat**	**Chol**	**Sodium**
	244	23g	18g	1g	9g	2g	94mg	145mg

Chicken Italiano

Serve with your favorite pasta

3/4 lb. chicken pieces, skinned, boned
2 green onions, chopped
1/2 cup tomato sauce
2 tablespoons chopped sun-dried tomatoes
1/4 cup vermouth or white wine
2 tablespoons chopped fresh parsley
Cooked pasta

Spray an Ultrex 10-inch nonstick sauté pan with olive oil cooking spray. Brown chicken; move pieces aside and stir-fry green onions. Remove skillet from heat and stir in remaining ingredients. Cover and simmer until chicken is done, about 15 minutes. Serve over cooked pasta. Makes 4 servings.

Each serving with white meat contains:	Cal	Prot	Carb	Fib	Tot. Fat	Sat. Fat	Chol	Sodium
	153	20g	4g	1g	5g	1g	49mg	244mg

Each serving with dark meat contains:	Cal	Prot	Carb	Fib	Tot. Fat	Sat. Fat	Chol	Sodium
	161	17g	4g	1g	7g	1g	70mg	262mg

Chicken & Lima Beans

A colorful stove-top casserole.

2 teaspoons canola oil
1 lb. chicken pieces, skinned, boned
1 garlic clove, minced
1/2 onion, chopped
1 (10-oz.) pkg. frozen lima beans
1 (16-oz.) can tomatoes with juice
2 teaspoons fresh chopped parsley
1/2 teaspoon paprika
Salt and pepper to taste

Heat oil in an Ultrex 12-inch nonstick sauté pan and brown chicken. Add garlic and onion, sauté. Add lima beans, tomatoes, parsley and paprika. Cover, reduce heat and simmer until chicken is done, about 15 minutes. Makes 6 servings.

Each serving with white meat contains:				Tot.	Sat.		
Cal	**Prot**	**Carb**	**Fib**	**Fat**	**Fat**	**Chol**	**Sodium**
167	22g	14g	5g	3g	0	44mg	186mg

Each serving with dark meat contains:				Tot.	Sat.		
Cal	**Prot**	**Carb**	**Fib**	**Fat**	**Fat**	**Chol**	**Sodium**
174	19g	14g	5g	5g	1g	63mg	202mg

Mandarin Chicken

Five-spice powder blends star anise, cinnamon, cloves, fennel (sweet anise) and Szechuan peppercorns.

2 teaspoons canola oil
3/4 lb. chicken pieces, skinned, boned
1 tablespoon low-sodium soy sauce
1/2 teaspoon five-spice powder
2/3 cup chicken broth or rice wine

Heat oil in an Ultrex 10-inch nonstick sauté pan, sauté chicken. Remove from heat. Add soy sauce and sprinkle with five-spice powder. Add broth or rice wine. Cook 5 to 7 minutes, turn and cook 8 to 10 minutes longer. Makes 4 servings.

Each serving with white meat contains:	**Cal**	**Prot**	**Carb**	**Fib**	Tot. **Fat**	Sat. **Fat**	**Chol**	**Sodium**
	162	21g	1g	0	8g	1g	49mg	313mg

Each serving with dark meat contains:	**Cal**	**Prot**	**Carb**	**Fib**	Tot. **Fat**	Sat. **Fat**	**Chol**	**Sodium**
	170	18g	1g	0	10g	1g	70mg	331mg

Variation

Substitute 1 tablespoon Worcestershire sauce for soy sauce and apple juice for broth. Add 1 apple, cut in eighths.

Mission Chicken Thighs

Superb flavor of rice dotted with vegetables complements the chicken.

2 slices bacon, chopped
1 cup uncooked long-grain white rice
1 small green or red bell pepper, chopped
1 small onion, chopped
1 cup chopped mushrooms (6 to 8 medium)
1 peeled carrot, finely chopped
1-1/2 cups chicken broth or stock
1/2 cup dry white wine
1/2 teaspoon salt
1/8 teaspoon pepper
2 teaspoons chopped fresh sage
6 chicken thighs, skinned
Paprika
Chopped parsley

In an Ultrex 10-inch nonstick sauté pan cook bacon until crisp. Stir in rice; cook and stir until rice begins to turn a light golden color. Add bell pepper, onion, mushrooms, carrot, stock or bouillon, wine, salt, pepper and sage. Stir until well mixed. Arrange chicken thighs on top; sprinkle with paprika. Cover and simmer 35 to 40 minutes or until chicken is done. Sprinkle with parsley at serving time. Makes 6 servings.

Each serving contains:	Cal	Prot	Carb	Fib	Tot. Fat	Sat. Fat	Chol	Sodium
	249	18g	29g	1g	4g	1g	59mg	278mg

Monterey Chicken Salad

A beautiful combination of colors and flavors.

3/4 cup cooked black beans, drained
1/2 cup chopped, peeled jícama
1/3 cup cooked peas
2 tablespoons chopped pimiento
3/4 cup cubed cooked chicken
1 banana, sliced
3 tablespoons orange juice
3 tablespoons canola oil
1 tablespoon fresh chopped cilantro
(Chinese parsley)
1 green onion, chopped
Salt and pepper to taste
Lettuce

Chill ingredients before combining. In an Ultrex large mixing bowl mix together beans, jícama, peas, pimiento, chicken and bananas. In a cup stir together orange juice, oil, cilantro and green onion. Pour over bean mixture. Gently toss. Season to taste with salt and pepper. Line a serving dish with lettuce leaves, top with bean mixture. Serve at once. Makes 6 servings.

Each serving with white meat contains:	**Cal**	**Prot**	**Carb**	**Fib**	Tot. **Fat**	Sat. **Fat**	**Chol**	**Sodium**
	164	11g	13g	3g	8g	1g	22mg	19mg

Each serving with dark meat contains:	**Cal**	**Prot**	**Carb**	**Fib**	Tot. **Fat**	Sat. **Fat**	**Chol**	**Sodium**
	177	10g	13g	3g	10g	1g	25mg	23mg

Chicken with Nectarines

Fresh peaches can be substituted for nectarines in this dish with an unusual combination of flavors.

2 tablespoons canola oil
1/2 onion, chopped
1 6-inch stalk lemon grass
1 lb. chicken pieces, skinned, boned
1/2 teaspoon garlic powder
2 cups passion fruit juice
1/4 teaspoon chili powder
1 tablespoon cornstarch
3 nectarines, pitted, sliced
4 teaspoons chopped cilantro
   (Chinese parsley) for garnish

Heat oil in an Ultrex 10-inch nonstick sauté pan and sauté onion and lemon grass. Add chicken and lightly brown. Sprinkle with garlic powder. Add 1 cup passion fruit juice and chili powder. Reduce heat, cover and cook over medium heat about 15 minutes. Mix cornstarch in remaining cup of passion fruit juice. Stir into skillet and cook until slightly thickened. Add nectarine slices. Cook about 5 minutes. Remove lemon grass. Serve chicken topped with nectarines and sauce. Garnish with chopped cilantro. Makes 4 servings.

Each serving with white meat contains:	Cal	Prot	Carb	Fib	Tot. Fat	Sat. Fat	Chol	Sodium
	312	28g	32g	3g	9g	1g	65mg	79mg
Each serving with dark meat contains:	Cal	Prot	Carb	Fib	Tot. Fat	Sat. Fat	Chol	Sodium
	323	24g	32g	3g	12g	2g	94mg	103mg

Chicken with Peaches

Fresh, ripe peaches made even better with a brandy sauce.

1/2 cup peach preserves
1/4 cup boiling water
1 tablespoon brandy or brandy flavoring
1 teaspoon catsup
2 teaspoons lemon or lime juice
1 teaspoon cornstarch
3/4 lb. chicken pieces, skinned, boned
2 fresh peaches, sliced, peeled

Spray baking dish with vegetable cooking spray. Set aside. Preheat oven to 375F (190C). In a small bowl combine peach preserves, boiling water, brandy, catsup, lemon or lime juice and cornstarch. Place chicken pieces in baking dish. Spoon sauce over. Bake uncovered, basting several times, about 30 minutes. Add peach slices, spoon some of the sauce over, continue baking 10 minutes. Makes 4 servings.

Each serving with white meat contains:	**Cal**	**Prot**	**Carb**	**Fib**	**Tot. Fat**	**Sat. Fat**	**Chol**	**Sodium**
	232	20g	35g	1g	1g	0	49mg	74mg

Each serving with dark meat contains:	**Cal**	**Prot**	**Carb**	**Fib**	**Tot. Fat**	**Sat. Fat**	**Chol**	**Sodium**
	240	17g	35g	1g	3g	1g	70mg	92mg

Orange Chicken Casserole

Serve with fresh asparagus or green beans.

1 cup uncooked long-grain white rice
1/2 cup chicken broth
2 cups orange juice
2 tablespoons dried currants
2 tablespoons chopped pistachios
3/4 lb. chicken breasts, skinned, boned
1/2 cup plain nonfat yogurt
1/2 teaspoon dried-leaf tarragon
Paprika
1 (11-oz.) can mandarin oranges, drained

Preheat oven to 350F (175C). Spray a shallow 2-quart baking dish with vegetable cooking spray. Spread rice evenly over bottom of dish. Combine chicken broth, orange juice, currants and pistachios in an Ultrex small mixing bowl. Pour over rice. Place chicken breast on top. Brush chicken with yogurt. Sprinkle with tarragon and paprika. Cover and bake about 30 minutes; uncover, add oranges and continue baking about 15 minutes until chicken is done. Makes 4 servings.

Each serving contains:	Cal	Prot	Carb	Fib	Tot. Fat	Sat. Fat	Chol	Sodium
	422	27g	69g	3g	4g	1g	50mg	85mg

Rosemary-Orange Chicken

An interesting blend of herbs and orange.

2 lb. chicken pieces, skinned
1/2 cup crushed cereal flakes
1 teaspoon crushed dried-leaf rosemary
1-1/2 teaspoons paprika
1-1/2 teaspoons grated orange peel
1 teaspoon ground oregano
3/4 cup evaporated skimmed milk

Remove all visible fat from chicken. Combine cereal, rosemary, paprika, orange peel and oregano in a pie plate or small paper bag. Pour milk in another pie plate. Spray a baking sheet with vegetable cooking spray. Preheat oven to 375F (190C). Dip each chicken piece into milk mixture and then into cereal mixture. Place coated pieces on prepared baking sheet. Bake 30 to 40 minutes. Makes 4 servings.

Each serving of white meat contains:	Cal	Prot	Carb	Fib	Tot. Fat	Sat. Fat	Chol	Sodium
	153	28g	5g	0	2g	0	66mg	112mg

Each serving with dark meat contains:	Cal	Prot	Carb	Fib	Tot. Fat	Sat. Fat	Chol	Sodium
	164	24g	5g	0	5g	1g	95mg	136mg

Chicken in Salsa Verde

Tomatillas resemble green tomatoes, but have a paper-like husk covering. They are also available canned.

**2 teaspoons canola oil
1 lb. chicken pieces, skinned, boned
1/2 onion, chopped
1 garlic clove, minced
1 lb. fresh or 1 (12-oz.) can tomatillas
3 whole roasted green chilies, chopped
1/2 cup apple juice
1 tablespoon fresh chopped cilantro
    (Chinese parsley)**

Spray an Ultrex 12-inch nonstick sauté pan with vegetable cooking spray. Heat oil and sauté chicken. Add onion and garlic, stirring until limp. Add remaining ingredients. Reduce heat, cover and simmer about 15 minutes. Makes 4 servings.

Each serving with white meat contains:	<u>Cal</u>	<u>Prot</u>	<u>Carb</u>	<u>Fib</u>	Tot. <u>Fat</u>	Sat. <u>Fat</u>	<u>Chol</u>	<u>Sodium</u>
	205	28g	14g	3g	4g	1g	65mg	87mg

Each serving with dark meat contains:	<u>Cal</u>	<u>Prot</u>	<u>Carb</u>	<u>Fib</u>	Tot. <u>Fat</u>	Sat. <u>Fat</u>	<u>Chol</u>	<u>Sodium</u>
	216	24g	14g	3g	7g	1g	94mg	111mg

Soft Chicken Tacos

No frying needed. For that south of the border flavor just heat and fill soft flour tortillas.

2 teaspoons canola oil
1/4 onion, chopped
1 cup chopped, cooked chicken
8 lard-free flour tortillas
1 cup Tomato Salsa, page 66
1/2 cup shredded Monterey Jack cheese
1 cup shredded lettuce
12 radishes, sliced

In an Ultrex 2-quart nonstick saucepan heat oil and sauté onion. Add chicken, cover and heat. Warm tortillas. Spoon chicken mixture on tortilla, top with Tomato Salsa, cheese, lettuce and radishes. Fold in half and serve. Makes 8 tacos.

Each taco with white meat contains:	Cal	Prot	Carb	Fib	Tot. Fat	Sat. Fat	Chol	Sodium
	191	10g	23g	2g	8g	3g	20mg	290mg

Each taco with dark meat contains:	Cal	Prot	Carb	Fib	Tot. Fat	Sat. Fat	Chol	Sodium
	197	9g	23g	2g	9g	3g	22mg	292mg

Ann's Tarragon Chicken

If fresh tarragon is available, use double the amount called for.

1/2 cup grated Parmesan cheese
1 tablespoon dried-leaf tarragon
1/2 teaspoon paprika
1/4 teaspoon white pepper
Dash garlic powder
Dash onion powder
3/4 lb. chicken pieces, skinned, boned

In an Ultrex small mixing bowl combine Parmesan cheese, tarragon leaves, paprika, white pepper and a dash of garlic powder and onion powder. Preheat oven to 350F (175C). Spray a baking dish with vegetable cooking spray. Spray chicken with vegetable cooking spray and then roll in Parmesan-cheese mixture. Place coated pieces in baking dish. Cover with foil and bake about 20 minutes. Uncover and continue baking 10 minutes until lightly browned. Makes 4 servings.

Each serving with white meat contains:	Cal	Prot	Carb	Fib	Tot. Fat	Sat. Fat	Chol	Sodium
	140	24g	1g	0	4g	2g	57mg	243mg

Each serving with dark meat contains:	Cal	Prot	Carb	Fib	Tot. Fat	Sat. Fat	Chol	Sodium
	148	21g	1g	0	6g	3g	78mg	261mg

Yakitori Chicken

Mirin can be found in the Oriental food section of your market.

Yakitori Sauce:
1/4 cup mirin (sweet rice wine)
3 tablespoons low-sodium soy sauce
1-1/2 teaspoons grated fresh ginger root
1 green onion, chopped
1 garlic clove, minced
1/4 teaspoon sesame oil

3/4 lb. chicken, skinned, boned, cubed

In an Ultrex medium mixing bowl combine Yakitori Sauce ingredients. Add cubed chicken and marinate at least 30 minutes. Thread chicken cubes on skewers. Broil 5 to 7 minutes, turning and brushing with marinade several times during cooking. Makes 4 servings.

Each serving with white meat contains:	Cal	Prot	Carb	Fib	Tot. Fat	Sat. Fat	Chol	Sodium
	126	20g	3g	0	1g	0	49mg	830mg

Each serving with dark meat contains:	Cal	Prot	Carb	Fib	Tot. Fat	Sat. Fat	Chol	Sodium
	135	18g	3g	0	4g	1g	70mg	848mg

Walnut Chicken Stir-Fry

A bit of chili sauce adds extra spice.

**1 egg white
1/2 lb. chicken, skinned, boned, cubed
2 tablespoons canola oil
2 teaspoons grated fresh ginger root
1 green onion, chopped
1 garlic clove, minced
1/2 cup sliced bamboo shoots
3/4 cup chopped walnuts
1/2 cup sliced water chestnuts
1 (6-oz.) pkg. frozen pea pods, thawed
3 tablespoons prepared chili sauce
2 teaspoons sugar
1 teaspoon sesame oil
2 tablespoons low-sodium soy sauce**

In an Ultrex small mixing bowl lightly beat egg white. Add chicken cubes, combine and set aside 10 minutes. In an Ultrex stir-fry pan or 12-inch nonstick fry pan heat oil, add ginger root, onion and garlic. Add chicken pieces and stir-fry until chicken is opaque, about 3 minutes. Add bamboo shoots, walnuts, water chestnuts and pea pods. Stir-fry 2 to 3 minutes. In a cup combine chili sauce, sugar, sesame oil and soy sauce. Stir chili-sauce mixture into chicken mixture to coat all pieces. Serve at once. Makes 4 servings.

Each serving with white meat contains:					Tot.	Sat.		
	Cal	**Prot**	**Carb**	**Fib**	**Fat**	**Fat**	**Chol**	**Sodium**
	346	22g	17g	4g	22g	2g	33mg	743mg

Each serving with dark meat contains:					Tot.	Sat.		
	Cal	**Prot**	**Carb**	**Fib**	**Fat**	**Fat**	**Chol**	**Sodium**
	351	21g	17g	4g	24g	2g	47mg	755mg

Turkey Burros

A simple Mexican dish that is becoming popular throughout the country.

2 teaspoons canola oil
1/2 cup chopped onions
2 cups cubed, cooked, skinned turkey
1/2 cup chopped green chiles
1 teaspoon dried-leaf oregano
1 large tomato, chopped
1/2 cup cooked peas
2 cups Tomato Salsa, page 66
12 (10-1/2-inch) flour tortillas
3/4 cup shredded Monterey Jack cheese

Heat oil in an Ultrex 2-quart nonstick saucepan, add onions and cook until softened. Stir in turkey, chiles, oregano, tomato, peas and 1 cup Tomato Salsa. Heat mixture and set aside. Dip each tortilla in 3/4 cup Tomato Salsa; set aside on a plate. Fill each tortilla with 3 tablespoons turkey mixture in a 13 x 9-inch baking dish. Roll and place seam side down. Pour remaining Tomato Salsa over filled burros. Sprinkle with cheese. Bake in a 350F (175C) oven about 20 minutes. Makes 12 burros.

Each burro with white meat contains:	Cal	Prot	Carb	Fib	Tot. Fat	Sat. Fat	Chol	Sodium
	265	14g	37g	3g	8g	2g	22mg	392mg

Each burro with dark meat contains:	Cal	Prot	Carb	Fib	Tot. Fat	Sat. Fat	Chol	Sodium
	272	14g	37g	3g	9g	3g	26mg	396mg

Favorite Turkey Chili

If you are an avid chile fan, you may want to increase the amount of chili powder.

1 tablespoon canola oil
1 lb. ground turkey
1 onion, chopped
1 clove garlic, crushed
3 large tomatoes, peeled and chopped
1 (8-oz.) can tomato sauce
1 tablespoon chili powder
1 tablespoon chopped fresh oregano
2 tablespoons chopped fresh cilantro
**   (Chinese parsley)**
1/2 teaspoon ground cumin
1/2 teaspoon salt
1 (29-oz.) can pinto or kidney beans, drained
1/4 cup plain nonfat yogurt
2 tablespoons chopped fresh cilantro for garnish

Heat oil in an Ultrex 5-1/2-quart nonstick saucepan. Add turkey and stir until crumbly. Add onion, garlic, tomatoes, tomato sauce, chili powder, oregano, 2 tablespoons cilantro, cumin and salt. Cover and cook on low for one hour. Add drained pinto or kidney beans. Cover and heat. Spoon into individual bowls. Top each serving with yogurt and additional cilantro. Makes 6 to 8 servings.

Each serving contains:	**Cal**	**Prot**	**Carb**	**Fib**	**Tot. Fat**	**Sat. Fat**	**Chol**	**Sodium**
	321	24g	34g	14g	11g	2g	39mg	373mg

Spicy Italian Turkey

Just the dish for that patio dinner.

4 (4-oz.) turkey breasts, skinned, boned
1 (8-oz.) can salt-free tomato sauce
1 teaspoon Italian seasoning
1/4 teaspoon chili powder
1/2 cup Italian seasoned breadcrumbs
1/4 cup grated Parmesan cheese
1/4 teaspoon chili powder

Cut turkey into bite-size cubes. In an Ultrex medium mixing bowl combine tomato sauce, Italian seasoning and 1/4 teaspoon chili powder. Add turkey, cover and refrigerate at least one hour. Preheat oven to 475F (245C). Combine breadcrumbs, cheese and chili powder. Drain turkey and roll in crumb mixture. Spray a shallow baking dish with olive oil vegetable cooking spray. Place coated turkey in a single layer in prepared dish. Spray top of turkey cubes with olive oil vegetable cooking spray. Bake uncovered about 8 minutes. Turn frequently while baking. Or thread cubes onto skewers and grill. Makes 4 servings.

Each serving contains:	Cal	Prot	Carb	Fib	Tot. Fat	Sat. Fat	Chol	Sodium
	223	30g	14g	1g	5g	2g	64mg	257mg

Singapore Turkey

For a spicier version increase chili powder or sprinkle with chile pepper flakes.

2 teaspoons canola oil
2 teaspoons grated ginger root
1 garlic clove, minced
1 green onion, chopped
1/4 teaspoon chili powder
2 teaspoons low-sodium soy sauce
1 tablespoon vinegar
2 teaspoons sugar
1 teaspoon cornstarch
1 (8-oz.) can pineapple slices in juice
1/2 cup reserved pineapple juice
3/4 lb. turkey breast cutlets
3 tablespoons all-purpose flour
1 tablespoon canola oil
Salt and pepper to taste

In an Ultrex 10-inch nonstick sauté pan, heat oil, sauté ginger root, garlic and green onion. Stir in chili powder, soy sauce, vinegar and sugar. Drain pineapple juice, adding additional water if necessary to make 1/2 cup. Dissolve cornstarch in pineapple juice, stir into mixture. Stir constantly until slightly thickened; cover and set aside. Sprinkle turkey cutlets with flour. In an Ultrex 12-inch nonstick fry pan, heat oil and sauté turkey. Add reserved sauce; cover and cook about 10 minutes. Season to taste with salt and pepper. Serve with pineapple slices. Makes 4 servings.

Each serving contains:	Cal	Prot	Carb	Fib	Tot. Fat	Sat. Fat	Chol	Sodium
	208	18g	17g	1g	8g	1g	39mg	211mg

California Chicken Sandwich

A combination of flavors that says, California!

2 slices sourdough bread
2 teaspoons Dijon-style mustard
1 tablespoon Green Chile Mayonnaise, page 57
3 oz. sliced, cooked chicken
1 lettuce leaf
1/2 tomato, sliced
1/4 avocado, thinly sliced
1/4 cup fresh alfalfa or bean sprouts

Lightly toast bread. Spread one slice of toasted bread with mustard. Spread another slice with Green Chile Mayonnaise. Top with lettuce, sliced chicken, tomato, avocado and alfalfa sprouts. Top with mustard-coated bread. Makes 1 sandwich.

Each sandwich with white meat contains:	Cal	Prot	Carb	Fib	Tot. Fat	Sat. Fat	Chol	Sodium
	433	33g	42g	8g	15g	3g	67mg	574mg

Each sandwich with dark meat contains:	Cal	Prot	Carb	Fib	Tot. Fat	Sat. Fat	Chol	Sodium
	470	30g	42g	8g	21g	5g	78g	585mg

Rosy Broiled Chicken Sandwich

The glossy marmalade topping creates a tempting look and flavor. Serve with fresh fruit slices.

4 teaspoons Dijon-style mustard
4 slices sourdough bread
4 spinach leaves
3/4 lb. sliced broiled chicken
4 tablespoons Tomato Marmalade, page 67

Spread mustard on one side of each slice of bread. Place fresh spinach leaves on top. Thinly slice broiled chicken. Spoon Tomato Marmalade on top. Makes 4 open-face sandwiches.

Each sandwich with white meat contains:	**Cal**	**Prot**	**Carb**	**Fib**	**Tot. Fat**	**Sat. Fat**	**Chol**	**Sodium**
	297	28g	38g	1g	3g	1g	65mg	324mg

Each sandwich with dark meat contains:	**Cal**	**Prot**	**Carb**	**Fib**	**Tot. Fat**	**Sat. Fat**	**Chol**	**Sodium**
	334	25g	38g	1g	9g	2g	76mg	335mg

Deviled Turkey Sandwiches

This filling can serve as a salad as well as a sandwich.

1 cup chopped cooked turkey
1/4 cup chopped celery
1 green onion, chopped
2 tablespoons chopped pickles
1 tablespoon chopped pimiento
1/2 teaspoon prepared horseradish
1/2 teaspoon Dijon-style mustard
2 tablespoons reduced-calorie mayonnaise
4 pita bread pockets
12 cherry tomatoes, halved
1 cucumber, sliced
4 lettuce leaves, shredded

In an Ultrex small mixing bowl mix together turkey, celery, green onion, pickles, pimiento, horseradish, mustard and mayonnaise. Cut pita breads in half, open pocket and fill with turkey mixture, tomatoes, cucumber and lettuce. Makes 4 sandwiches.

Each sandwich with white meat contains:	**Cal**	**Prot**	**Carb**	**Fib**	**Tot. Fat**	**Sat. Fat**	**Chol**	**Sodium**
	275	18g	43g	3g	4g	1g	26mg	476mg

Each sandwich with dark meat contains:	**Cal**	**Prot**	**Carb**	**Fib**	**Tot. Fat**	**Sat. Fat**	**Chol**	**Sodium**
	286	18g	43g	3g	5g	1g	32mg	482mg

Barbecued Turkey Burgers

For added flavor brush burgers with barbecue sauce while broiling.

3/4 lb. ground turkey
1/4 cup rice bran
2 tablespoons bottled barbecue sauce
1 teaspoon Dijon-style mustard
1 green onion, chopped
4 hamburger buns
4 teaspoons reduced-calorie mayonnaise
4 slices lowfat Cheddar cheese
Lettuce

In an Ultrex medium mixing bowl combine turkey, rice bran, barbecue sauce, mustard and green onion. Shape into 4 burgers. Broil 7 to 10 minutes per side or until cooked through. Lightly spread mayonnaise on buns. Top with burger, cheese and lettuce. Makes 4 burgers.

Each burger contains:	Cal	Prot	Carb	Fib	Tot. Fat	Sat. Fat	Chol	Sodium
	451	34g	28g	3g	21g	7g	80mg	649m

Desserts

From the time we were children, dessert has always been a reward for being good. This might have been anything from eating your vegetables to a special occasion or the arrival of visitors. Rich, calorie-laden treats were anticipated.

We can still look forward to the final touch of a lovely meal without feeling guilty.

I emphasize using fresh fruits because their fresh flavors and bright colors are enticing. Some require a little more time for preparation, while picture-pretty Stuffed Plums can be prepared in minutes. By combining fruits and berries in Blueberry Plum Pudding, the familiar cobbler takes on a new look. Apricot Pudding transforms plain bread into a delicious dessert by including apricots and almonds, topped with a great sauce.

Sliced fruit accompanied by an Apricot, Lemon or Cherry Sauce changes ordinary into extraordinary.

I have not forgotten chocolate is probably the favorite dessert flavor. Use cocoa powder, rather than solid chocolate which is high in fat, and you can still enjoy treats like Minted Pears with Chocolate Sauce or Chocolate Cherry Shortcake.

My favorites have always been frozen desserts. That craving is satisfied beautifully with frozen yogurt. Most of the time my guests never guess they're eating yogurt and not ice cream. Serve with Chocolate Snowballs and be prepared to offer seconds.

Papaya Raspberry Pie or Blackberry-Lemon Bars are just the thing to serve with a pot of brisk tea.

It is increasingly difficult to buy ripe produce, so plan to purchase produce in ample time to allow for ripening.

Art Krull's TV Marshmallow Treats

Art is known far and wide for making these treats on the Home Shopping Network. His expert advice is "Don't spill this on the burners!"

2 tablespoons butter or lowfat diet margarine
1 (8-oz.) bag miniature marshmallows
6 cups Rice Krispies®

In an Ultrex 3-quart nonstick saucepan melt the butter or margarine over low heat. Add marshmallows; heat, stirring gently until melted. Add Rice Krispies and thoroughly mix. Let cool for a few minutes. Spray a 9 x 9 baking pan with cooking spray; press the partly cooled marshmallow mixture gently into the pan. Allow to finish cooling, then cut into squares. Makes 16 small servings

Each serving with butter contains:	Cal	Prot	Carb	Fib	Tot. Fat	Sat. Fat	Chol	Sodium
	99	1gg	21g	0	2g	1g	4mg	99mg

Each serving with lowfat diet margarine contains:	Cal	Prot	Carb	Fib	Tot. Fat	Sat. Fat	Chol	Sodium
	98	1g	21g	0	1g	0	0	90mg

Blackberry-Lemon Bars

A pretty three-layer cookie to satisfy your sweet tooth.

2 tablespoons diet margarine
1/2 cup nonfat cream cheese
2 teaspoons lemon peel
3/4 cup packed brown sugar
1 cup self-rising flour
3/4 cup egg substitute or 6 egg whites
1/2 cup sugar
4 teaspoons lemon juice
1/2 teaspoon vanilla extract
1 teaspoon baking powder
3 tablespoons all-purpose flour
1/2 cup seedless blackberry or black raspberry jam
Powdered sugar

Preheat oven to 350F (175C). In a mixer bowl combine margarine, cream cheese, lemon peel and brown sugar. Add self-rising flour and thoroughly combine. Spray an 8-inch square baking dish with vegetable cooking spray. Pat mixture into bottom and bake 15 minutes. In a mixer bowl beat egg substitute or egg whites until frothy, gradually add sugar. Continue beating until lightly thickened. Fold in lemon juice, vanilla, baking powder and all-purpose flour. Remove baking dish from oven and spread jam on surface. Slowly pour lemon mixture over jam. Return to oven and bake another 20 minutes. Cool 15 minutes before sifting powdered sugar over all. Cool another 10 minutes before cutting into slices. Makes 20 bars.

Each bar contains:	Cal	Prot	Carb	Fib	Tot. Fat	Sat. Fat	Chol	Sodium
	113	2g	25g	0	1g	0	0	135mg

Chocolate Snowballs

Treats that are crunchy on the outside and chewy in the middle.

2 egg whites, room temperature
1/4 teaspoon cream of tartar
1/2 cup sugar
2 tablespoons unsweetened cocoa powder
1/4 cup finely chopped candied red cherries
2 tablespoons finely chopped walnuts

Line 2 cookie sheets with brown paper: set aside. Preheat oven to 275F (135C). In a medium mixer bowl beat egg whites and cream of tartar until foamy. Gradually add sugar, beat until very stiff and glossy. Sift cocoa over mixture, beat until blended. Stir in candied cherries and walnuts. Spoon slightly rounded tablespoons of mixture onto lined cookie sheets, about 2 inches apart. Bake 35 minutes in preheated oven. Turn off oven; leave cookies in closed oven for 1 hour. Makes 25 to 30 cookies.

Each cookie contains:	**Cal**	**Prot**	**Carb**	**Fib**	**Tot. Fat**	**Sat. Fat**	**Chol**	**Sodium**
	24	0	5g	0	0	0	0	9mg

Variation
Omit cocoa, cherries and walnuts. Substitute 1/2 cup chopped dried fruit, 1/2 teaspoon almond extract and 1/2 cup crisp rice cereal.

Frozen Yogurt Pie

The Graham Crumb Crust is the ideal base for this frozen yogurt pie.

Graham Crumb Crust:
1-1/2 cup graham cracker crumbs
2 teaspoons cocoa powder
3 tablespoons nonfat plain yogurt
2 tablespoons packed brown sugar

1 recipe Peaches & Cream Frozen Yogurt, page 210
2 fresh peaches, peeled, sliced for garnish

In an Ultrex medium mixing bowl combine all crust ingredients. Press crumb mixture into a 9-inch pie shell. Bake in a 350F (175C) oven 5 minutes. Cool. Fill with frozen yogurt, smoothing top evenly. Cover with plastic wrap and freeze until ready to serve. Garnish with fresh peach slices. Makes 1 (9-inch) pie (6 servings).

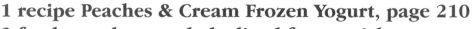

Each serving contains:	Cal	Prot	Carb	Fib	Tot. Fat	Sat. Fat	Chol	Sodium
	339	9g	71g	3g	4g	1g	2mg	271mg

Oil Pastry

Easy to mix and easy to roll.

2-1/4 cups all-purpose flour
1/4 teaspoon salt
1/2 cup canola oil
2 teaspoons vinegar
4 to 5 tablespoons ice water

In an Ultrex medium mixing bowl mix together flour and salt. Make a well in center. Pour in oil, vinegar and water. Stir together with a fork until ingredients are combined. Form into 2 balls, flatten slightly. Cover with plastic wrap and chill 30 minutes. Place 1 ball between two sheets of waxed paper. Roll out into 10-inch circle. Remove one sheet of waxed paper. Fit into pie plate; remove other piece of waxed paper. Flute or crimp edges of crust. Bake unfilled crust in 475F (245C) oven about 10 minutes. For a double-crust pie, fit pastry into pie pan, fill as desired and top with second crust. Seal edges together. Bake according to recipe. Makes 2 (9-inch) pie shells (12 servings).

Each serving contains:	**Cal**	**Prot**	**Carb**	**Fib**	**Tot. Fat**	**Sat. Fat**	**Chol**	**Sodium**
	166	2g	18g	1g	9g	1g	0	45mg

Papaya Raspberry Pie

Fresh fruits are hidden beneath a golden meringue.

1 (9-inch) Oil Pastry crust, page 193, baked
1 tablespoon raspberry liqueur or extract
3 tablespoons raspberry jam
1 to 2 ripe papayas, sliced, peeled and seeded
1 cup raspberries
4 egg whites
1/2 cup sugar

Preheat oven to 350F (175C). Heat raspberry liqueur or extract and jam. Brush on cooled baked pie crust. Place papaya slices in a pinwheel design, starting from center. Sprinkle with raspberries. Beat egg whites in an Ultrex medium mixing bowl until foamy. Gradually add sugar and continue beating until stiff and glossy. Spread over fruit filling. Seal meringue to edge of crust. Bake about 15 minutes until golden brown. Remove and cool before serving. Makes 6 servings.

Each serving contains:	Cal	Prot	Carb	Fib	Tot. Fat	Sat. Fat	Chol	Sodium
	298	5g	49g	3g	10g	1g	0mg	84mg

Lemon-Date Tart

A pleasing combination of the tart lemon in a date-sweetened crust.

3 egg whites
3/4 cup sugar
1 teaspoon baking powder
1/2 cup crushed soda crackers
1/2 cup chopped dates
1/3 cup chopped walnuts
1/3 cup sugar
3 tablespoons cornstarch
1/2 cup egg substitute
1 tablespoon grated lemon peel
1/3 cup lemon juice
2/3 cup water

Preheat oven to 325F (165C). Spray a 9-inch pie plate with vegetable cooking spray. Set aside. In a mixer bowl beat egg whites until frothy, continue beating and gradually add sugar. Beat until stiff peaks form, beat in baking powder. Fold in cracker crumbs, dates and walnuts. Spread mixture in prepared pie pan. Bake about 25 minutes, until lightly browned. In a saucepan combine sugar and cornstarch. Stir in egg substitute, lemon peel, lemon juice and water. Cook over medium heat, stirring constantly, until thickened, 5 to 7 minutes. Remove from heat. When crust is baked, remove from oven and let cool 10 minutes. Carefully press center down, making a 1/2-inch thick edge. Spoon lemon filling into depressed area. Smooth the surface evenly. Cool and refrigerate before serving. Makes 8 servings.

Each serving contains:	Cal	Prot	Carb	Fib	Tot. Fat	Sat. Fat	Chol	Sodium
	211	5g	42g	1g	4g	0	1mg	140mg

Chocolate Cherry Shortcake

Thaw frozen cherries and drain canned cherries before using.

3/4 cup water
1/3 cup nonfat dry milk
1/3 cup sugar
3 (1-gram) packets Sweet'n Low® sugar substitute
2 tablespoons unsweetened cocoa powder
2 teaspoons cornstarch
1/2 teaspoon vanilla extract
2 teaspoons margarine or butter
1 tablespoon orange-flavored or almond-flavored liqueur
12 oz. pitted fresh, frozen or canned dark sweet cherries
1 (6- to 7-inch) angel food loaf cake, cut crosswise
   into 8 equal slices
1/2 cup frozen "lite" nondairy whipped topping

In a small bowl combine water and dry milk; stir until milk dissolves. Set aside. In an Ultrex 1-quart nonstick saucepan combine sugar, sugar substitute, cocoa powder and cornstarch; stir until well blended. Add milk; cook and stir over medium-low heat until mixture begins to boil. Reduce heat; simmer and stir 6 or 7 minutes more, or until slightly thickened. Remove from heat. Add vanilla, margarine or butter and liqueur, if desired. Stir until margarine or butter is melted and blended into mixture. Stir in cherries. Cover surface of mixture with plastic film. Cool to room temperature; then refrigerate until serving time. Spoon chocolate-cherry mixture over cake slices. Top each slice with 1 tablespoon whipped topping. Makes 8 servings.

Each serving contains:	Cal	Prot	Carb	Fib	Tot. Fat	Sat. Fat	Chol	Sodium
	219	5g	46g	1g	3g	1g	0	298mg

Marshmallow-Surprise Cupcakes

Light in texture, delicious in flavor.

4 egg whites, beaten
1/3 cup nonfat milk
1/3 cup canola oil
3/4 cup grated zucchini
2 tablespoons unsweetened cocoa powder
1 cup all-purpose flour
1/4 cup oat bran
1/2 cup sugar
2 teaspoons baking powder
1 teaspoon ground cinnamon
1/2 teaspoon ground nutmeg
1 teaspoon vanilla extract
1/2 cup chopped miniature marshmallows
1/4 cup chopped walnuts

Preheat oven to 375F (190C). Line muffin pan cups with paper baking cups or spray with vegetable cooking spray; set aside. In an Ultrex large mixing bowl fold together egg whites, milk, oil and zucchini. Add cocoa, flour, oat bran, sugar, baking powder, cinnamon, nutmeg and vanilla. Mix together until dry ingredients are moistened, batter will be lumpy. Spoon 1 tablespoon batter into each muffin cup. Combine marshmallows and nuts. Spoon evenly over batter in muffin cups. Top with remaining batter. Bake 15 to 18 minutes. Remove from pan; cool 5 minutes and serve. Makes 12 large cupcakes.

Each cupcake contains:	**Cal**	**Prot**	**Carb**	**Fib**	**Tot. Fat**	**Sat. Fat**	**Chol**	**Sodium**
	162	4g	21g	1g	8g	1g	0	80mg

Blueberry Plum Pudding

A superb combination of fruits. If you prefer, use blackberries or boysenberries.

1 (16-oz.) pkg. frozen blueberries
1/2 cup sugar
4 teaspoons cornstarch
4 teaspoons lemon juice
4 plums, sliced, pitted
1/2 cup egg substitute or 4 egg whites
1/4 cup sugar
1 tablespoon grated lemon peel
1 teaspoon vanilla extract
1/2 cup all-purpose flour

Spray a 6-cup baking dish with butter-flavor vegetable cooking spray. Set aside. Preheat oven to 325F (165C). Place frozen blueberries in an Ultrex 2-quart nonstick saucepan to defrost. Blend 1/2 cup sugar with cornstarch, lemon juice and blueberries. Cook, stirring constantly over medium heat until slightly thickened. Place plums in prepared baking dish. Pour blueberry mixture over plums. In a mixer bowl beat egg substitute or egg whites and gradually add 1/4 cup sugar and lemon peel. Fold in vanilla and flour. Spoon over fruit and bake uncovered about 40 minutes. Serve warm. Makes 6 servings.

Each serving contains:	Cal	Prot	Carb	Fib	Tot. Fat	Sat. Fat	Chol	Sodium
	252	4g	58g	3g	2g	0	0	44mg

Grandma's Maple-Nut Tapioca

An old-fashioned dessert with a modern touch.

3 cups water
1-1/2 cups packed dark-brown sugar
1/2 cup tapioca
1 tablespoon unsweetened cocoa powder
1 teaspoon vanilla extract
1/3 cup chopped walnuts
1/3 cup plain nonfat yogurt

In an Ultrex 3-quart saucepan combine water, brown sugar, tapioca and cocoa. Cook stirring constantly, about 10 minutes until mixture thickens and tapioca becomes transparent. Remove from heat and stir in vanilla and walnuts. Spoon into 6 bowls and refrigerate. To serve, top with yogurt. Makes 6 servings.

Each serving contains:	Cal	Prot	Carb	Fib	Tot. Fat	Sat. Fat	Chol	Sodium
	299	3g	67g	1g	4g	0	0	34mg

Apricot Pudding

A wonderful dish to make with leftover bread.

1 (14-oz.) can sweetened condensed milk
1 (14-oz.) can orange juice
2 egg whites, beaten
1/2 teaspoon almond extract
1 tablespoon grated orange peel
3 cups cubed bread
1 (16-oz.) can apricots, chopped, drained
1/3 cup toasted almonds, chopped
Apricot Sauce, page 207

Preheat oven to 350F (175C). Spray a 2-quart baking dish with butter flavored vegetable cooking spray. Pour condensed milk into an Ultrex large mixing bowl. Pour orange juice into milk can; pour juice into condensed milk, stir to blend. Fold in egg whites, almond extract and orange peel. Add bread, apricots and almonds, fold to coat all ingredients. Let stand 5 minutes; pour into prepared dish. Place a shallow pan of water on lower oven rack. Place baking dish on rack above. Bake uncovered 35 to 40 minutes. Top will be lightly browned. Remove and cool 10 minutes. Serve topped with Apricot Sauce. Makes 9 servings.

	<u>Cal</u>	<u>Prot</u>	<u>Carb</u>	<u>Fib</u>	Tot. <u>Fat</u>	Sat. <u>Fat</u>	<u>Chol</u>	<u>Sodium</u>
Each serving contains:	284	8g	48g	2g	7g	3g	15mg	207mg

Baked Apple Delight

A warm breakfast or dessert to serve on a cold day.

Prune-Currant Sauce:
1 tablespoon cornstarch
1 cup apple juice
1 cup pitted prunes
1/4 cup dried currants
3 tablespoons brown sugar
1/4 teaspoon ground cloves
1 teaspoon lemon peel
2 tablespoons lemon juice
1/4 cup pecans, chopped

4 large baking apples

For Prune-Currant Sauce:
In an Ultrex 1-quart nonstick saucepan blend cornstarch with apple juice. Add remaining ingredients and cook, stirring constantly until sauce thickens.

For Baked Apple Delight:
Core apples and peel tops about 1 inch. Place in a shallow baking dish. Fill each cavity with Prune-Currant Sauce, reserve any remaining sauce. Bake at 350F (175C) about 60 minutes, until apples are tender. Heat remaining sauce and spoon additional sauce over baked apples. Serve warm. Makes 4 servings.

Each serving contains:	__Cal__	__Prot__	__Carb__	__Fib__	Tot. __Fat__	Sat. __Fat__	__Chol__	__Sodium__
	377	3g	86g	11g	6g	1g	0	11mg

Fruit Salad Dessert

What could be simpler? Slice your fresh fruit and top it with a delicious touch of honey.

4 fresh figs, quartered
2 oranges, peeled, sliced
24 red cherries
24 green grapes
1 Granny Smith apple, sliced

Honey-Pecan Sauce:
1/4 cup honey
3/4 cup plain nonfat yogurt
2 tablespoons orange juice
1 teaspoon orange peel, grated
2 tablespoons pecans, toasted

Arrange fruit in an attractive pattern on each plate. In a small bowl combine honey, yogurt, orange juice and orange peel. Drizzle Honey-Pecan Sauce over fruit, sprinkle with pecans. Makes 4 servings.

Each serving contains:	Cal	Prot	Carb	Fib	Tot. Fat	Sat. Fat	Chol	Sodium
	254	5g	57g	6g	4g	0	1mg	35mg

Minted Pears
with Chocolate Sauce

*Glamorize this easy-to-make, reduced-calorie, classic
dessert with a sprinkling of chopped walnuts.*

4 fresh pears
2 cups water
3/4 cup sugar
2 tablespoons coarsely chopped fresh mint leaves
6 drops green food coloring
2 tablespoons unsweetened cocoa powder
1/4 cup water
1/4 cup sugar
1/4 cup light corn syrup
1 tablespoon margarine
4 scoops lowfat frozen vanilla yogurt
4 teaspoons finely chopped walnuts

Peel, halve and core pears. In an Ultrex 10-inch nonstick sauté pan
combine 2 cups water, 3/4 cup sugar, mint leaves and green food
coloring. Bring to a boil. Drop in pears and simmer 5 minutes; turn over
in syrup and simmer another 2 or 3 minutes, or until tender. Remove
from heat; refrigerate in syrup. Combine cocoa powder, 1/4 cup water,
1/4 cup sugar and corn syrup in small saucepan. Stir constantly over low
heat until well blended. Simmer 2 minutes, stirring occasionally. Add
margarine; set aside to cool. Drain chilled pears; discard mint leaves and
liquid. Place a scoop of frozen yogurt in center of each of 4 pear halves.
Top with remaining pear halves, forming 4 whole stuffed pears. Spoon
about 1 tablespoon chocolate sauce into each of 4 dessert dishes. Stand
1 whole stuffed pear on end in chocolate sauce in each dessert dish.
Spoon remaining chocolate sauce over each. Sprinkle with nuts. Makes
4 servings.

Each serving contains:	<u>Cal</u>	<u>Prot</u>	<u>Carb</u>	<u>Fib</u>	Tot. <u>Fat</u>	Sat. <u>Fat</u>	<u>Chol</u>	<u>Sodium</u>
	465	5g	106g	6g	5g	1g	15mg	92mg

Stuffed Plums

Contrasting textures, flavors and colors create a great dessert or snack.

1/4 cup nonfat cream cheese
1 tablespoon lime or orange marmalade
2 teaspoons chopped crystallized ginger
4 plums
4 teaspoons chopped pistachio nuts

In a small bowl thoroughly combine cream cheese, marmalade and ginger. Slice plums in half, set aside. Fill each plum half with cream-cheese mixture and sprinkle with nuts. Makes 4 servings.

Each serving contains:	Cal	Prot	Carb	Fib	Tot. Fat	Sat. Fat	Chol	Sodium
	72	2g	14g	2g	2g	0	0	7mg

Variation
Substitute fresh apricots or peaches for plums.

Baked Puffs

Fill these golden puffs with salad, fruit or frozen yogurt.

1/2 cup water
1/4 cup canola oil
1/2 cup all-purpose flour
1/4 teaspoon salt
1/2 cup egg substitute
Fruited Cheese Filling, page 206
Powdered sugar

Spray a cookie sheet with butter-flavor cooking spray. Set aside. Preheat oven to 425F (220C). In an Ultrex 2-quart nonstick saucepan heat water and oil to boiling. Add flour and salt all at once. Stir vigorously until flour combines making a ball. Remove from heat; let stand 5 minutes. Beat in one-half egg substitute. When thoroughly combined, beat in remaining amount. Drop by tablespoonfuls or pipe into 1-1/2-inch mounds on prepared sheet. Bake about 25 minutes until puffs are browned and appear dry. Remove and cool. Slice tops off, remove any excess inside shells. Fill with Fruited Cheese Filling. Replace top, sprinkle with powdered sugar. Makes 10 (3-inch) puffs.

	Cal	**Prot**	**Carb**	**Fib**	**Tot. Fat**	**Sat. Fat**	**Chol**	**Sodium**
Each puff contains:	82	2g	5g	0	6g	0	0	78mg

Fruited Cheese Filling

Use as a filling for Baked Puffs, page 205, or crepes. Great on pancakes.

1 cup cream-style, lowfat cottage cheese
2 tablespoons sugar
4 teaspoons orange liqueur or juice
1/2 teaspoon vanilla extract
2/3 cup blueberries, blackberries or strawberries
3 tablespoons chopped pistachios

In a food processor, blender or mixer, combine cottage cheese, sugar, orange liqueur or juice and vanilla. Process until smooth. Rinse berries and place on paper towels, pat dry. Spoon mixture into a bowl and fold in nuts and berries. Makes about 2 cups.

Each tablespoon contains:	Cal	Prot	Carb	Fib	Tot. Fat	Sat. Fat	Chol	Sodium
	15	1g	2g	0	0	0	0	29mg

Apricot Sauce

A delicious topping for Apricot Pudding, page 200.

4 oz. dried apricots
3/4 cup apple juice
1/2 cup orange juice
1/4 cup honey
2 tablespoons water
2 teaspoons cornstarch
Ground ginger to taste
Ground cinnamon to taste
1 tablespoon sweet vermouth

Cover apricots with apple juice in an Ultrex 1-quart nonstick saucepan. Bring to a full boil, then reduce heat and simmer, covered, 30 minutes. Stir apricots occasionally so they will not stick or burn. Let apricots cool, then strain. Reserve cooking liquid. Chop cooked apricots and set aside. In an Ultrex 2-quart nonstick saucepan combine orange juice, honey, water, cornstarch, ginger and cinnamon. Heat, stirring constantly, until thickened slightly. Remove pan from heat and add apricots, their cooking liquid and vermouth. Serve hot or well chilled. Makes 1-1/2 cups.

	Cal	**Prot**	**Carb**	**Fib**	**Tot. Fat**	**Sat. Fat**	**Chol**	**Sodium**
Each tablespoon contains:	30	0	8g	0	0	0	0	1mg

Cherry Sauce

Brighten angel-food cake or frozen yogurt with a special flavor.

1/3 cup sugar
1-1/2 tablespoons cornstarch
1/4 teaspoon ground allspice
1 (16-oz.) can tart pie cherries, pitted
1/4 cup sliced almonds
1/2 teaspoon almond extract
2 to 3 drops red food coloring

In an Ultrex 2-quart nonstick saucepan combine sugar, cornstarch and allspice. Drain liquid from cherries. Set aside. Slowly stir cherry liquid into sugar mixture. Cook over medium heat, stirring constantly, 5 to 7 minutes until slightly thickened. Add cherries and almonds; cook 2 to 3 more minutes. Remove from heat and add almond extract and food coloring. Makes about 1-1/2 cups.

Each tablespoon contains:	Cal	Prot	Carb	Fib	Tot. Fat	Sat. Fat	Chol	Sodium
	25	0	5g	0	1g	0	0	2mg

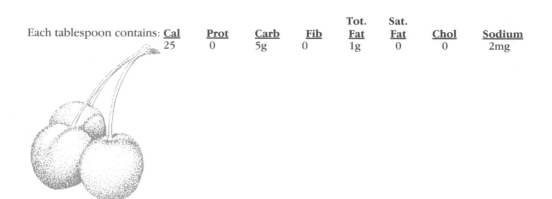

Peppermint-Stick Chocolate Mold

Angel food loaves vary in length and weight. If you have extra cake, freeze it for another time.

6 (3/4-inch-thick) crosswise slices of angel food cake
1 envelope unflavored gelatin
2 tablespoons cold water
3/4 cup sugar
3 tablespoons unsweetened cocoa powder
1/2 cup nonfat milk
1/4 cup crushed peppermint sticks or Starlight mints
1 cup plain nonfat yogurt, stirred
2 egg whites
1/8 teaspoon cream of tartar

Cut each cake slice into 3 strips about 1-1/4 x 2-3/4 x 3/4 inches. Line bottom of 8-inch springform pan with 1/2 the cake strips forming a spoke pattern. Set aside remaining strips. Sprinkle gelatin over water; let stand at least 1 minute. In an Ultrex 2-quart nonstick saucepan combine sugar and cocoa, add milk. Stir over moderate heat until smooth. Mix in dissolved gelatin. Set aside to cool about 10 minutes. Reserve 1 tablespoon crushed peppermint; add remaining candy to cocoa mixture. Stir into yogurt. Refrigerate until partially set. Beat egg whites in an Ultrex small mixing bowl until foamy; add cream of tartar. Beat until stiff but not dry. Fold into chocolate mixture. Spoon over cake in pan. Top with reserved cake strips in a spoke pattern. Lightly press strips until they are partially covered with chocolate mixture. Refrigerate until firm. Carefully remove sides of pan; sprinkle top with reserved peppermint. Makes one (8-inch) mold.

Each serving contains:	Cal	Prot	Carb	Fib	Tot. Fat	Sat. Fat	Chol	Sodium
	227	7g	51g	1g	1g	0	1mg	248mg

Peaches & Cream Frozen Yogurt

This will become a summertime favorite with a new twist.

1 lb. fresh or 1 (1-lb.) pkg. frozen peaches, thawed
1 tablespoon cream sherry
1/2 cup honey
1 cup nonfat yogurt
1 cup evaporated skimmed milk
8 strawberries for garnish
Mint leaf for garnish

In a blender or food processor, purée peaches with cream sherry and honey. Stir in yogurt and evaporated milk. Freeze in ice-cream maker according to manufacturer's directions. Serve cold with garnish of strawberries or mint leaf. Makes 8 servings.

Each serving contains:	<u>Cal</u>	<u>Prot</u>	<u>Carb</u>	<u>Fib</u>	Tot. <u>Fat</u>	Sat. <u>Fat</u>	<u>Chol</u>	<u>Sodium</u>
	132	4g	30g	1g	0	0	2mg	60mg

Strawberry Banana Frozen Yogurt

Treat yourself: Use any fresh or frozen fruit that you like.

1 cup nonfat plain yogurt
1 cup nonfat milk
1/4 cup light corn syrup
1/4 cup egg substitute
1 banana
1 (10-oz.) pkg. frozen strawberries

Combine all ingredients in blender or food processor. Pour into a freezer container. For individual servings, pour into 8 (4-oz.) paper cups. Cover and freeze until firm. For a smoother texture, break into pieces and place in a mixer bowl, blender or food processor. Blend until fluffy. Makes 1 quart.

Each serving contains:	Cal	Prot	Carb	Fib	Tot. Fat	Sat. Fat	Chol	Sodium
	87	4g	18g	1g	0	0	1mg	59mg

Variation
Lemon Supreme:
Omit corn syrup, banana and fruit; increase egg substitute to 1 cup, add 3/4 cup sugar, 1 tablespoon lemon peel, 1/3 cup lemon juice and 1 (12-oz.) can frozen juice concentrate.

Peach Melba:
Omit egg substitute and banana. Substitute 1-1/2 cups puréed peaches and use frozen raspberries.

Index